Leadership Secrets For Healthcare

Volume I: Developing Self-Leadership In Others

by:

S. L. Bartow

S. L. Bartow

Copyright © 2011 by S. L. Bartow. All Rights Reserved.

Except as permitted under the US Copyright Act of 1976, no part of this publication may be reproduced, distributed or transmitted in any form or by any means or stored in a database or retrieval system without the prior written permission of the Author.

Printed in the Unites States of America
First Printing: September 2011
ISBN: 978-1441435880

This publication is designed to provide accurate and authoritative information in regard to the subject matter covered. It is sold with the understanding that neither the author nor the publisher is engaged in rendering legal, accounting, or other professional service. If legal advice or other expert assistance is required, the services of a competent professional person should be sought.
> *- From a Declaration of Principles jointly adopted by a Committee of the American Bar Association and a Committee of Publishers.*

A production of:
MAXnJAX Media & BLAST Leadership Systems

For more information please visit:
MAXnJAX.com/leadership

CONTENTS

PREFACE vii

ACKNOWLEDGMENTS ix

Chapter 1 1
Why It's Called Work
Business Before Pleasure

Chapter 2 3
Why There Are Management Problems
People Make Things Happen
Managing Constant Change
The Better Approach

Chapter 3 7
Real Life In The Manager's World
The Ultimate Challenge
Divide And Conquer Problems
Sub-Divide Into Smaller Problems

Chapter 4 13
Accomplishing More With Less
Considering Self-Leadership
Big Results – Little Effort

Chapter 5 17
Two Types Of People
The Books And Their Covers

Chapter 6 19
Two Types of Management Style
Management Through Osmosis
Manager VS Leader

Chapter 7 23
Accomplishing Work And Objectives
What Is Catastrophism?
Avoiding Catastrophism

Chapter 8 25
Acknowledge Success In Others
It's Not A Popularity Contest
Be Genuine And Sincere
Fear Of Leadership
Believing In People
Opportunity For Others To Succeed

Chapter 9 31
The Leadership Frame Of Mind

Chapter 10 33
First Things First
Don't Assume Anything

Chapter 11 35
Establish A Clear Vision

Chapter 12 37
Effective Goal Setting
Direction For Desired Results
Clearly Establish And Record Goals
Keep Goals Simply Defined
Unique Circumstances And Situations

Chapter 13 43
Ownership And Commitment
Clearly Define Expectations
Get Commitment And Ownership

Chapter 14 45
Involving Everyone In The Plan
Stay Focused In Spite Of Change
Communicate Effectively

Chapter 15 47
Providing Appropriate Feedback
Opportunities For Positive Change
Timing Is Everything

Chapter 16 .... **51**
Managers Who Watch And Ding
Positive Reinforcement
Praise In Public
Give Praise When And Where It's Due

Chapter 17 .... **55**
Kindness Is Not Weakness
Identifying Alpha Employees
Dealing With Alpha Employees

Chapter 18 .... **57**
Identifying Performance Problems
Treating Causes, Not Symptoms

Chapter 19 .... **59**
Reprimanding Poor Performance
Positive Results Through Reprimands
Being The Mechanism Of Performance
Make Decisions Based Upon Facts
Leading Others To Self-Discovery
Self-Induced Reprimands
Avoid Comparisons To Others
Don't Muddy The Water

Chapter 20 .... **67**
Proper Aptitude And Attitude Are Essential
Can They Do The Job?
Will They Do The Job?

Chapter 21 .... **69**
The Two "Can't" Rules
Providing Resources Needed To Succeed
Choices And Consequences
Getting Past The Problem
Reprimand The Behavior, Not The Person
Document Disciplinary Actions
Have A Witness
Value And Worth

Chapter 22 77
Being Fair And Consistent
Keeping Your Game Face On
Employee Benefits Are Crucial
Pay Reviews, Raises, And Promotions
Creating A Better Work Environment

Chapter 23 85
The Need For Champions
Championing A Cause
Look Before You Leap
Political Considerations

Chapter 24 89
Training And Development
Who's Training Who?
Correcting Bad Habits

Chapter 25 93
Leading By Example

Chapter 26 95
Demotions, Reassignments, And Terminations
Unavoidable Changes In Employment
Job Status Options
Risk / Reward Ratio
Corrective Action Options

Chapter 27 101
Don't Be The Party Pooper
Let Go Of Control And Constraint

Chapter 28 103
To Save Or Not To Save, That Is The Question
Consistency In Performance Standards
A Common Mistake
Monitoring New Employee Performance
The Cost Of Keeping Under-Achievers
Cutting Your Losses

Chapter 29 111
Deciding To Replace Employees
When To Replace Employees
How To Replace Employees
Protecting The Organization's Interests

Chapter 30 115
Dealing With Time Wasters
Others Who Waste Your Time
Redirecting And Penalizing Time Wasters
Non-Confrontational Redirection

Chapter 31 121
Working With PRN Employees
Working With Agency / Temp Employees
Consider Temps For Full Time
Pros And Cons Of Temps

Chapter 32 125
Simplifying The Recruiting Process
Advertising, Marketing, And Networking
Fishing For Results
Cost Effective Advertising
Accepting Applications

Chapter 33 129
Conducting Effective Interviews
Using An Interview Checklist
The Two Parts Of An Interview
Focus On Critical Factors
The Mechanics of Interviewing
Digging For Information
During The Interview
Ask The Right Questions
Don't Be Naive
After The Interview
Don't Promise Anything Just Yet
The Second Interview
Choose Your Words Carefully
Making The Employment Offer
Prerequisites To Hiring

Chapter 34 145
Benefiting From Employee Input And Feedback
Positively Spinning Feedback
Appreciate The Extra Effort
Soliciting Employee Input And Feedback
Giving Feedback On The Feedback
Input And Feedback On A Personal Level
Using Suggestion Boxes Effectively
Admitting Problems Is Not Failure
Conducting Effective Exit Interviews
Look For Ways To Improve
Don't Ask Unless You're Prepared To Address It

Chapter 35 157
Lady Justice Is Blind, You Shouldn't Be
Don't Let Your Guard Down
Leading A Horse To Water
Gaining Greater Knowledge And Understanding

Chapter 36 161
Put And Keep The Odds In Your Favor
Don't Rely On Luck
Divide And Conquer Your Dreams
Employee Satisfaction
Greatness Or Just Average

CONCLUSION 165

WHAT'S NEXT? 167

APPENDIX A – Part I 169

APPENDIX A – Part II 185

PREFACE

In most other industries, managers are responsible for managing / supervising groups of people and are hired specifically for those positions. However, in the healthcare industry, simply being a charge nurse puts you in a position of management / supervision over other people, sometimes several people (i.e. trainees, Med Techs, aides, etc.).

From CEOs to charge nurses, employment in healthcare will involve and require management skills at every level. Whether you want to be a manager or not, it's a virtual certainty that you will. Unfortunately, for the most part, people in the healthcare industry are not properly trained for managerial responsibilities.

Because of this lack of training on an industry-wide basis, it would be beneficial to you to have some knowledge and understanding of how to best succeed with the people you manage / supervise.

Whether you're a seasoned veteran CEO or a brand new charge nurse with your first day on the floor, this book will help you. More importantly, it will help you help those around you, in providing a better workplace.

Most management books are written specifically for professional managers and tend to exclude everyone who isn't exclusively in a management position (i.e. department heads, charge nurses, etc.).

This book is written specifically for the unique managerial and supervisory challenges faced in the healthcare industry at every level. Because healthcare is so demanding and challenging, the principles contained in this book can be universally applied to almost any other industry with equally beneficial results.

This book focuses mainly on people skills and development. After all, it's people who are responsible for getting everything done in the workplace. People are the greatest resource in any organization and ultimately the best place to invest.

ACKNOWLEDGMENTS

I began writing this book as a resource for the employees for whom I have managerial / supervisory responsibilities. It became clear early on that having a resource such as this book would be invaluable for getting me and my staff "singing from the same sheet of music."

I have many years of experience in the healthcare industry, much of it spent in management and leadership positions. I'm very fortunate to have been associated with many excellent mentors and role models over the years. They have shared their collective experiences, wisdom and insights into the discipline of management and leadership, along with people skills, organizational skills, and developing self-leadership in others. Without them, this book would not have been possible.

I have always had a desire to help others, which explains my career path into the healthcare industry. It is my further desire to help not only the patients / residents, but also the caregivers. I want to share the knowledge and secrets that I know in helping others to not only help themselves, but those around them as well, to enjoy a better, more fulfilling and rewarding life.

I also want to thank my entire family for their love, support, and encouragement. Life is much better when you are surrounded by people who always have your best interests at heart and support you in whatever you do.

Finally, I want to thank all the people I've had the pleasure of associating myself with in the healthcare industry. My growth, not only as a leader and mentor, but also as a person, have been shaped by my experiences and interactions with many, many wonderful people.

Chapter 1

Why It's Called Work

I'll never forget my first day of bona fide employment. I got a job at a fast food restaurant my senior year of high school. It was an eight hour shift on a busy Saturday and I earned every penny of my wages that day. I was completely worn out by the time my shift ended.

When it was finally time to go home, the manager wanted to visit with me to review how the day had gone. The first question he asked was, "So, how was your first day?" All I could think of was how hard I had worked, how much my feet ached and how demanding the job was. The words that came out of my mouth were, "It sure was a lot of work."

The manager chuckled and said, "That's why they call it *work*. If it was fun, people would get up in the morning and say that they had to go to *fun*!" That's why you never hear anyone say they're going to fun, because work usually isn't a lot of fun- it's almost always a lot of work!"

> You never hear anyone say they're going to fun, because work usually isn't a lot of fun- it's almost always a lot of work!

I know you've heard the old saying, "find a job you love and you'll never have to work another day in your life." Well, I can assure you that I absolutely love my job and the people with whom I associate. However, at the end of the day, I've never been able to rationalize in my mind that the 8 to 10 hours of time (often very laborious) that I just put in wasn't a lot of work.

I like to share this with new employees, especially those for whom it may be their first bona fide job. I have found that it is beneficial for them to sit down and discuss the issue of work, why it's called work and not called fun. They need to have a clear understanding of what is involved and the amount of effort that's required to get the job done.

Working in healthcare is one of the most stressful jobs a person can have. It's not like making widgets, where there's a certain amount of "down time," between production runs. The patients aren't on any production run or schedule. Their needs may be varied, but often demanding of everyone's time and focus.

Business Before Pleasure
Having said that, it doesn't mean that work can't involve fun or be fun at times. You've heard it said before, "business comes before pleasure," and business almost always involves work.

I have found over the years that the only way to combine business with pleasure is through discipline. No, not *disciplinary action*, but rather through personal discipline and a strong work ethic of all the people involved in the work being done.

> The only way to combine business with pleasure is through discipline.

If everyone is disciplined enough to get the job done correctly and on time, then they've earned the right to have a commensurate amount of fun, so long as it's proper, isn't wasting time and doesn't interfere with the business at hand. However, having fun should never be the reason for not getting the job done correctly and on time or neglecting customer (i.e. patients, residents, etc.) needs and service.

Chapter 2

Why There Are Management Problems
One of the biggest problems with management and leadership training in healthcare is that at worst, it's virtually non-existent and at best, it's often ineffective.

To compound the problem even more, there's little, if any focus on continuing management and leadership training once you get a job with supervisory responsibilities and have to start making decisions involving other people. It can be both intimidating and frustrating when you have responsibilities for other people and their results, and you're not quite sure how to deal with those responsibilities positively and effectively.

> In healthcare, there's little, if any focus on continuing management and leadership training.

Today, many people are in supervisory positions that require managerial and leadership expertise, who have never studied management. For those who have had some formal management education, the information they gleaned from textbooks is often full of definitions and theories, but short of any real applications of effective management and leadership that is relative to today's work environment.

People Make Things Happen
In any given industry, a manager or leader's success will be the result of their people, because it is ultimately the people who make things happen. In fact, one of the largest mega-mart empires in the entire world insists that what makes a difference in their success is simply, their people. Sure, there are machines, all kinds of technology and gadgets, but without the people who know how to use them, they're nothing more than inanimate and useless objects.

In the healthcare industry the sole purpose of the entire industry revolves around people. From the employees to the services offered and provided, to the patients / residents (even their family members), it's all about people. It's easy then to see that there is a real need for valuable knowledge and proven techniques when it comes to dealing with other people in a positive, constructive and rewarding manner.

> There is a real need for valuable knowledge and proven techniques.

The ultimate goal of any organization is to provide a quality experience for their customers and consumers. This is especially important where there is competition. When competition is considered, organizations not only want their customers to have a quality experience, but they want it to be better than what the competition can provide. If this is true, then shouldn't the management and leadership of the organization be directed at employee improvement, in order to improve the customer experience?

Managing Constant Change

Another thing to consider is that the healthcare industry continuously operates in a state of flux. Things are constantly changing, whether it's new techniques, practices, procedures, regulations, etc., or just the fact that patient / resident loads and their needs change daily, if not more often.

Because of the constant changing nature of business, it is even more important for managers and leaders to utilize the most effective tools and resources available. Tools and resources that will facilitate the interaction and direction of the people for whom they have responsibility, in a productive, efficient, positive, and successful manner.

The Better Approach
Therein lies the purpose of this book. The wisdom and secrets found herein are a hybrid version of various disciplines of successful, proven management and leadership techniques. This book highlights the best of traditional management styles and techniques, while focusing on the benefits of effective leadership in helping others to become self-directing.

This book does not provide every answer to every question or problem that may arise. Instead, it provides a methodology and mentality of achieving the best possible results from the people who are most able to achieve those results. It provides an easily adaptable system to achieve success for both new managers / leaders as well as seasoned veterans alike. Which, when used appropriately and applied generously and consistently will yield bigger and better results with less time and effort.

While this book is intended primarily for the managerial (i.e. anyone with supervisory / management responsibilities) personnel, it can benefit everyone in the organization.

It doesn't matter whether you're the CEO, a mid-level manager, Administrator, DON, ADON, Charge Nurse, Department Head, or an entry level front line employee. It doesn't matter whether you are responsible for hundreds of people, a handful of people or just yourself- this book will help you work more efficiently and effectively with others around you.

The application of these principles and practices is simple, straightforward and can be adapted for virtually any situation and implemented in virtually any team, department, organization, etc.

PLEASE NOTE: Throughout this book I use the phrases "your employees" and "your people" somewhat interchangeably. Regardless of whether the person(s) you're supervising are your employees or just the people you're responsible for that shift, the principles are the same.

Chapter 3

Real Life In The Manager's World
In a perfect world a manager's job would be easy. It would involve reviewing the day's schedule and generally overseeing the operations. There would be meetings with other senior and junior level managers over coffee and donuts or lunch at a nice restaurant, courtesy of a vendor or sales representative.

In the real world, a manager's job is rarely, if ever like this. The day is usually full of obstacles, challenges, problems and demands that more often than not, can't be accomplished in a single day. Many managers don't even have time to sit down for lunch. They either have to eat on the run or skip lunch altogether in order to get more work done.

Numerous books have been written regarding the plight of managers with metaphorical images of swampy and murky mires, sharks, alligators, crocodiles, firefighters, armies, swords, shotguns, etc., none of which are pleasant. There's an entire industry devoted to audio and visual stimuli, books, tapes, DVDs, gadgets and gimmicks to help managers de-stress, re-focus, and press on. Clearly, the role of the typical manager can be extremely difficult and exhausting.

The Ultimate Challenge
It is ultimately the manager's responsibility to accomplish the goals and objectives of the organization with the resources available (including human resources), while maintaining standards. Those goals and objectives become the challenge or the problem for which the manager must find a solution. This can seem insurmountable or even impossible at times.

The typical manager spends countless hours, days, weeks, and even months or years trying to solve problems. Often, the results do not adequately meet the expectations. This leads to more negativity in the form of anxiety, stress, and frustration. The negativity often spills over to the employees in the form of irritation, anger and often outright contempt, which only exacerbates the situation.

> The typical manager spends countless hours, days, weeks, and even months or years trying to solve problems.

When this point is reached, it creates a vicious cycle of poor performance, poor quality, poor attitudes, poor communication, poor morale, poor products and services, and ultimately a poor experience for the customer. Not only does this affect the manager and their employees, but it extends upward, often to the highest levels of the organization. Once it reaches the top, it can have a trickle-down effect that negatively impacts everyone involved (see Chart UH-1).

Chart UH-1

As mentioned previously, the biggest problem managers face is the realization of the goals and objectives of the organization with the resources available to them. This is much more easily stated than accomplished.

Divide And Conquer Problems
A typical pit that many managers fall into is that "they can't see the trees for the forest." I know you've heard it said just the opposite. But *not being able to see the trees for the forest* implies that someone is so focused on the enormity of the forest (i.e. challenges, problems, etc.) that they fail to see the individual trees (i.e. the smaller problems that make up the bigger problem).

It's like the riddle, "how do you eat an elephant?" The answer is simply, "one bite at a time." It's the same way you would clear a forest- one tree at a time. It's how battles in the past were fought and won. In order to win, the prevailing army would find a way to split up or divide the enemy troops into smaller groups and systematically attack the smaller groups. This approach to solving problems and winning battles is known as the "divide and conquer" method.

In a very real way, this book is an example of the divide and conquer method. It is one of a series of books that will address virtually every aspect of effective management and leadership. This book is not intended to be an all-inclusive management and leadership solution, but rather the solution to specific and defined elements thereof.

> The divide and conquer method of solving problems consists of taking the problem (obstacle, challenge, etc.), regardless of its size and dividing it into smaller, more manageable pieces.

In business, the divide and conquer method of solving problems consists of taking the problem (obstacle, challenge, etc.), regardless of its size and dividing it into smaller, more manageable pieces. Then, if any of the smaller pieces cannot be easily managed, they are further divided into smaller sub-pieces.

By way of example, let's take a common problem – low employee morale. Employee morale in and of itself is not the problem, but rather the symptom of the problem. If we divide and conquer employee morale, it might look something like the following pie chart (Chart EMP-1).

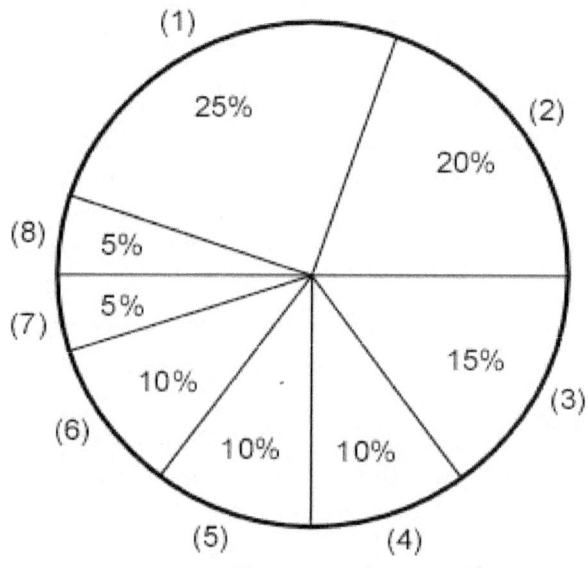

(1) Poor Management
(2) Unappreciated
(3) No Teamwork
(4) Understaffed
(5) Not Trained Properly
(6) Short of Supplies
(7) Low Wages
(8) Poor Benefits

Chart EMP-1

If you look at each of the pieces of the problem, you can probably see that most of the pieces could be further divided into smaller sub-problems. For example, the biggest factor contributing to low employee morale in this example is "poor management." That may be a suitable title to identify that particular part of the overall problem, but what does that really mean? How do you go about solving poor management?

The answer is simple, you have to further *sub-divide* and conquer each piece where it is necessary and practical to do so. We'll take "poor management" and further divide it in the following chart (Chart EMP-2).

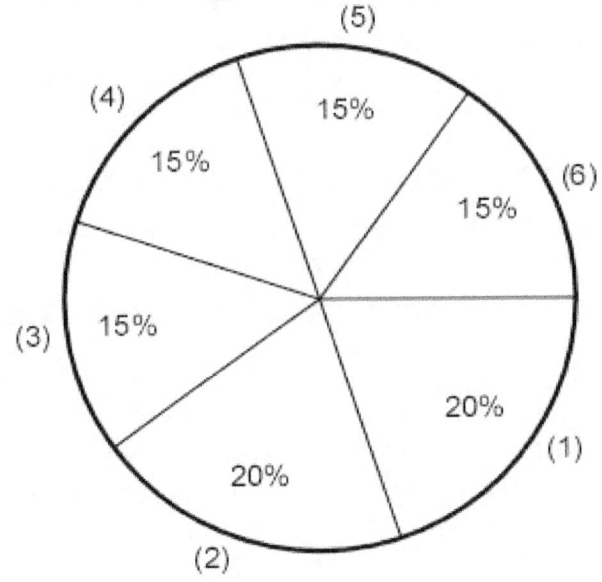

Chart EMP-2

Sub-Divide Into Smaller Problems

As you can see, the problem of "poor management" is not simply one problem, but a set of various quantifiable sub-problems. In this example, you could take some of these pieces and further sub-divide them as needed to get to the real root of the problem.

For instance, one of the biggest factors in this example is that the management is "unapproachable." What are the underlying factors that make the management team seem unapproachable to the employees? Once you've identified all the root causes, they can be addressed individually, in a more manageable way.

The dividing of any piece (problem) or sub-piece (sub-problem) can continue to be divided into as many sub-levels of smaller pieces (problems) that is necessary to properly manage and resolve it. The beauty of this method and process is that as you solve the smaller problems, the larger problems become solved along the way.

> As you solve the smaller problems, the larger problems become solved along the way.

Obviously, as you divide the bigger problems into smaller, sub-level problems, some will have a higher priority of resolution than others. As with everything else that involves managing and decision making, the most important matters should be addressed first and all others categorized by importance or relevance, pursuant to the desired goals and objectives.

Chapter 4

Accomplishing More With Less
Another barrier that stands in the path of many managers is that they simply lack the proper knowledge to effectively accomplish greater results with the resources they've been given. Quite often they rely upon the same old methods or systems of the past.

Unless you're happy with the results of the past and don't want to do better in the future, you're going to have to come up with a better plan. There's a saying, "if you always do what you always did, you'll always get what you always got." Albert Einstein defined it this way, "Insanity is doing the same thing over and over again and expecting different results."

> Insanity is doing the same thing over and over again and expecting different results.

One thing that managers often rely upon to reduce their work load and contribute to accomplishing more is through the delegation of responsibilities to others.

Delegation is simply the process of assigning work, duties, goals, responsibilities, etc. to the person who has (or should have) ownership for its completion. If no person has that particular ownership, then it should be delegated in such a way that it has the most favorable affect and benefit, not only to the organization, but the people involved as well.

Managers who fail to effectively delegate are left with the responsibilities and ownership of everything not properly delegated. They usually have a gigantic list of tasks that need to be accomplished throughout the day. They constantly check up on their employees to see what progress they're making.

While this type of management might get a certain amount of work accomplished and temporarily increase production, it isn't an effective, long-term strategy. This is especially obvious if this type of manager misses a day of work or more. Without the constant directing and redirecting, the employees would have little or no direction and productivity would suffer as a result.

A more effective strategy for delegation would be to assign the various work to the employees, giving them responsibility and accountability for their accomplishment. This is affectionately known as having the employees "take ownership" of their jobs. The manager would then only need to follow up periodically to make sure that the work was being accomplished, redirecting when and where necessary.

Considering Self-Leadership

However, the most effective strategy for accomplishing more results and better results consists less of delegation and more of developing self-leadership in others. Doing so results in having more people who are self-directed and lead themselves to the assumption of responsibilities and the effective completion of them.

No, I'm not suggesting that you simply let everyone in the organization do what they believe needs to be done, cross your fingers and hope that everything goes well and you'll get the results you're looking for. Doing that would be to abandon responsible management and leadership altogether.

What I am suggesting is that you adopt the style of management and leadership contained in this book, where you develop and foster self-leadership in others.

By doing so, the time you spend managing will be reduced to only what is needed or the situation requires. This will allow you to focus on your other responsibilities without neglecting the employees for whom you have supervisory responsibilities and obligations.

Who knows, you may even free up additional time for you to plan, develop strategies, keep up with your industry and engage in other activities that will help you "stay on top of your game."

Developing self-leadership in others allows you to accomplish more with less effort. It provides you with the ability to balance the work load, responsibilities, etc. It establishes certain safeguards and preventive measures that reduces future problems by reducing or eliminating the smaller factors that lead to problems in the first place. It's much like the saying, "a stitch in time saves nine."

> Developing self-leadership in others allows you to accomplish more with less effort.

Big Results – Little Effort
One of the biggest benefits of developing self-leadership is that it provides a better quality of life. Not only is it better for you, but for everyone else in the organization. Not only will morale improve, but you'll also see improvements in productivity, absenteeism and turn over. Customer Service will improve, as will the products and/or services that you provide. As such, you will be able to get very big results through people with very little time and effort expended.

It doesn't matter whether your business employs one person or thousands of people. It doesn't matter what industry you're in or the product or service you provide. It's the people who are ultimately responsible for getting things accomplished.

When people are happy and feel good about themselves, they naturally produce better results. Clearly, better results are the impetus of any management or leadership function. If better results can be accomplished in a way that is "neater, sweeter and more completer," with no down-side and lots of up-side, it really is a "no-brainer."

The concept of developing self-leadership in others involves believing in people and helping them to manage themselves and their lives in a more positive and productive way. When people are empowered to take ownership in their work world, they enjoy life more, are less stressed and ultimately more productive. No mater how you slice it, that's a win-win for everyone.

Chapter 5

Two Types Of People
There are basically two types of people in this world as it relates to the work environment. First, there are those people who only want to be there because they need a job and the money that goes along with it. To these people, work is simply a means to the end.

People like this are almost never progressing towards success in any significant way and are usually under-achievers. It's hard to imagine any situation where these type of people would be desirable for your organization.

The Books And Their Covers
However, in saying that, "you should never judge a book by its cover." Just because someone *appears* to be an under-achiever doesn't necessarily make it so. Sometimes the one thing that keeps people from being achievers is the right environment.

> Just because someone *appears* to be an under-achiever doesn't necessarily make it so.

It's quite simple, if you provide an environment that fosters success, those who want success in their life will rise up, just as cream rises to the top of milk.

Secondly, there are others who are already achievers who are presently successful in their job performances. You may even have some of these people in your organization. These people, along with those who truly want to do better will become the achievers. These are the people you can look to, who will add more to the success of your organization.

From my experience and the collective wisdom of other successful leaders, the under-achievers typically remain at the bottom. For this reason, the focus of this book is in dealing with the achievers and not the under-achievers. When you begin to apply the principles of effective leadership, the division of achievers from under-achievers will quickly become obvious to you.

This division of people into the two different groups will give you the opportunity to improve the overall organization by increasing achievement and success while reducing under-achievement.

You've probably hear it said that, "sometimes less is more." Whether you re-train under-achievers to become achievers or replace under-achievers with achievers, the end result is that your organization is better off with fewer under-achievers.

> With under-achievers, less is more.

There's always an argument between the cost / benefits of re-training people rather than removing and replacing them. It really comes down to the issue of training. If they weren't trained properly and the only thing keeping them from excelling is simply training, then by all means invest in re-training.

However, if training is not the real issue of the heart of the matter, then it must be attitude, aptitude or a combination of both, which will be discussed in greater detail later in this book.

Chapter 6

Two Types Of Management Style
There are typically two different types of management style. There's the serious, hard-nosed, by-the-book managers who focus so much on the bottom line that they usually forget or neglect to take into consideration the people who are actually doing the work. They're autocratic and taken to an extreme, they seem almost dictatorial in their actions and attitude.

Then there's the laid-back, casual managers who are interested in maintaining a friendly environment. They tend to focus more on people, often at the expense of the company and the bottom line. They tend to be more democratic and in extreme cases, they're less interested in managing and more interested in "people pleasing."

Some managers may find themselves somewhere in between, with characteristics from both management styles. Some managers may try to find a balance between both styles. With a little self-analysis, you may see yourself as falling into one of these two general categories.

Management Through Osmosis
Because there is little emphasis in managerial training in most healthcare organizations, most of what managers and supervisory people know they learned from their surroundings, such as at home or school. Still other characteristics may come from on-the-job experiences, trial-and-error, sticking with something that seems to work or simply something that has worked in the past for them or someone else.

Regardless of what influenced your style of management, being like either one of these two types of manager is at best, being only half a manager. It would stand to reason then that a whole manager would be both serious about the business and the bottom line, while fostering a people-friendly work environment. Clearly, being a whole manager is much more advantageous to everyone, rather than just half a manager.

Manager VS Leader

However, there is a better way, and that's being an effective leader. An effective leader is not only a whole manager, but cultivates a workforce of people who are successful self-leaders. Their people are focused on the company goals and objectives, while managing themselves in an environment that is the most productive for them. This can be illustrated in the following chart (Chart TM-EL).

Typical Managers	Effective Leaders
Bosses people, gives orders, makes demands, discourages independent thinking	Empowers people, provides direction, gives choices, encourages self-leadership
Makes rules to restrict people	Sets goals to liberate people
Finds fault with others, criticizes	Looks for good in others, praises
Sees things from own perspective, limited vision	Sees things from all perspectives, clear vision
Reactive to problems as they occur	Proactive in anticipating and preventing problems
Solves problems	Creates solutions
Focuses on conformity and methods	Focuses on achievements and results
Maintains status quo	Accomplishes vision, goals, and mission
Satisfied with meeting expectations	Striving for higher standards
Focuses on the immediate work load, problems and conditions	Focuses on today's issues and the future, utilizes critical thinking time

Typical Managers	Effective Leaders
Occupied with routine activities in day-to-day operations, takes on additional work	Accomplishes tasks through others, takes time for encouraging and empowering others
Confined with existing resources	Effectively utilizes current resources, acquires additional resources as needed
Works long hours, never has enough time	Works only necessary hours, makes time as needed, when needed
Thinks "inside the box"	Thinks "outside the box"
Asks, "why?"	Asks, "why not?"

Chart TM-EL

Chapter 7

Accomplishing Work And Objectives
As with the two types of management styles, there are typically two approaches that people take toward accomplishing work and objectives. The first type of approach is that of being reactive. A reactive manager waits until there is a problem and then reacts to the problem to provide a fix. You've heard the saying, "if it ain't broke, don't fix it."

This approach involves a lot of chance. The reactive manager is taking the chance that there won't be any problems or that when there are, they won't be so big that they can't be easily fixed. The reactive manager's focus doesn't change much until a problem arises that necessitates a fix.

What Is Catastrophism?
Unfortunately, this type of management typically leads to catastrophism. Catastrophism in business can be defined as changes being brought about by significant and often violent occurrences or reactions to events.

> Catastrophism: changes being brought about by significant and often violent occurrences or reactions to events.

This can be better illustrated in nature. For example, some scientists believe the Grand Canyon is the result of sudden catastrophic events rather than erosion over a long period of time.

If you've ever worked for a company (i.e. not self employed), you've probably witnessed catastrophism to some degree. It probably resulted in significant changes in the workplace and likely involved the removal of one or more persons from their jobs.

Avoiding Catastrophism

The other type of approach is that of being proactive. Being proactive is the process of providing stimulus that has an effect on events. It involves acting in advance and taking appropriate or necessary steps to prevent future problems. It is a process of anticipating problems that may occur and then devising methods or procedures in advance, in order to avoid problems from occurring at a later time.

Being a proactive manager provides a greater level of control over their environment and the outcome of their efforts. This provides the assurance that there won't be any surprises at a later time, and certainly no catastrophism.

It is the process of guiding the work and taking the appropriate actions that lead to results that match the desired and anticipated outcome. It involves cognitive thinking and being able to visualize how current actions in the workplace may affect it in the future.

An effective leader will take a proactive approach to all the necessary tasks, duties, assignments, goals and objectives. A proactive manager will also foster and expect the same from everyone else in the group, affording them the same benefits in their respective positions.

> An effective leader will take
> a proactive approach to all the necessary tasks,
> duties, assignments, goals and objectives.

Chapter 8

Acknowledge Success In Others
An effective leader knows that success breeds more success. Helping other people build upon their successes produces even more success.

In order to foster success, you have to be looking for it. You've probably heard it said that, "if you think you can or you can't, you're right." The same thing holds true for other people as well. Have you ever known of someone who was constantly told that they were good for nothing and in time that's exactly what they became?!

It's Not A Popularity Contest
Praising success is not a popularity contest, neither for your employees nor yourself. No matter what you do or how you do it, there will always be people who won't like you, what you're doing or how you're doing it. Abraham Lincoln observed that, "you can please some of the people all of the time, all the people some of the time, but you can never please all the people all of the time."

Praise that is earned and deserved is not about trying to be popular or please others. It's about recognizing success in others. It is openly acknowledging the efforts and achievements of others who deserve to be recognized.

> Look for opportunities to compliment someone for having done something successfully.

Look for opportunities to compliment someone for having done something successfully. When people are acknowledged for being successful, they will want to be more successful and will try even harder.

On the other hand, seeing only the failures in a person will only worsen that person's confidence, attitude and performance. That's not to say that you should reward someone for bad results. Kudos should only be given when earned, but when they are earned, don't hesitate to acknowledge success.

Be Genuine And Sincere
Be genuine and sincere when acknowledging others' success. Be happy for them. Be happy for yourself, because the more success they have, the more success you will have. Let them know how good it makes you feel seeing them do well. This will reinforce the fact that when they are successful, you're on their side, and you're both on the same team.

In years gone by, it was customary when someone accomplished something noteworthy that they would get a pat on the back from the boss. The better they had done, the heartier the pat on the back. Sadly, in today's litigious world I would recommend that you dispense with the physical displays of appreciation and stick with a verbal acknowledgment that is clearly genuine and sincere.

Fear Of Leadership
Being an effective leader doesn't happen overnight. For most managers, it's a little unsettling to wrap their minds around the concept that they are going to empower their employees to supervise themselves.

In extreme cases, some managers are engaged in micro-management, where they control even the smallest details of a person's job. It is especially difficult for a micro-manager to transition to an effective leader, but is possible with determination and effort.

Then there are other managers who will be afraid to embrace this concept and style of leadership out of fear. They fear that if they don't keep their thumbs on top of people and ride roughshod over them, one of them might actually excel and be noticed. They believe that if that happens, it will make them look bad and the employee look better and maybe even take their place as the manager.

And that's if only one person excelled. Can you imagine the fear this type of manager would feel if they anticipated that several people might excel and do better?! Why, they'd be petrified, because in their minds, their job would be in jeopardy from all their successful employees. It's like that phenomenon where there is a bucket of crabs, if one tries to crawl out, the others pull them right back in.

Believing In People
This is where the "believing in people" part comes into play. First you have to believe in yourself and have the confidence in knowing that if you help others excel, you can't help but excel in the process. You can get what you want in life faster and easier by helping others get what they want, especially if what you want must be derived through others.

> You can get what you want in life faster & easier by helping others get what they want.

Again, I'm not suggesting that one day you have your thumbs on everybody and the next day you tell everyone they're responsible for themselves. What I am saying is that you have to start, even if it's just a little at a time.

It may be best to visualize it at first and imagine the success playing out in your mind's eye. You've probably heard it said before that, "whatever the mind of man can conceive and believe, it can achieve."

This isn't just an experiment. What I'm suggesting has been done successfully by many managers and leaders with various backgrounds, from various walks of life and in various industries.

The first principle of success is to start with something that has the best potential to give you the return that you're looking for. In this case, you're looking for a return of not only improved performance, but people who can work independently towards established goals and objectives, who have a significant degree of self-discipline.

Opportunity For Others To Succeed

While it may seem that only your top performers may be suitable candidates for this process, don't rule out anyone just yet. Not everyone is going to be capable of leading themselves to better performance and productivity.

There are some people who will always need someone else directing them. These people are the exception rather than the rule, because the vast majority of people are capable of managing their own lives. For most people, they simply haven't been given the opportunity.

Without reservation, everyone in your organization should be given the opportunity to manage and lead themselves within the confines of realistic parameters. You'll never know and your people will never know what their full potential is until they have the opportunity to reach it.

> You'll never know
> and your people will never know
> what their full potential is until they have
> the opportunity to reach it.

And isn't that really what leadership is all about? In fact, true leadership, effective leadership, will produce more independent self-leaders and reduce the number of *dependent* followers.

Leadership isn't so much about what you can accomplish by yourself or how good you can make yourself look through your own efforts. It's about cultivating self-leaders and *allowing* them to accomplish more than you ever could.

> True leadership is about cultivating
> self-leaders and *allowing* them
> to accomplish more than you ever could.

Chapter 9

The Leadership Frame Of Mind
Getting started may involve more from you than from your employees. Because this is more about leadership than it is about management, you've got to get in the leadership frame of mind.

In essence, management involves the organization and coordination of the activities of an organization in accordance with certain policies and in achievement of clearly defined objectives. Management is often included as a factor of production along with machines, materials, and money. In a nutshell, management is about the manager controlling things to reach the goals.

On the other hand, leadership involves a clear vision of the desired outcome or results. It requires communicating that vision with others and providing the information, knowledge, and other resources necessary to realize the vision. In a nutshell, leadership is about getting others to participate and *creatively* utilize available resources to reach the desired results.

> Leadership is about getting others
> to participate and *creatively* utilize
> available resources to reach the desired results.

Before we continue, a few thoughts about creativity. Allowing or even encouraging creativity can go a long way in overall job satisfaction, reducing problems, increasing productivity and creating a better work environment for everyone.

However, in saying that, creativity should never affect the operation negatively or be allowed to happen haphazardly. I would suggest that all creative ideas be approved first before being randomly implemented by anyone.

Everything, including creativity should be implemented in a systematic and organized manner. The workplace should not be an experimental laboratory full of mad scientists.

Chapter 10

First Things First
While that might seem a bit over simplified, it's always best to start at the beginning. If you've ever witnessed someone trying to assemble a child's toy without reading the instructions, you'll have an idea of what I'm talking about. If you don't start at the beginning of the instructions, either something ends up not fitting right or you're left with unused parts. In most cases, the toy has to be disassembled and put back together according to the instructions.

The beginning, in the case of management and leadership is making sure that everyone has a clear understanding and knowledge of their specific job functions and duties. In addition, they need to have been properly trained in their specific job and have access to necessary resources.

It's unreasonable and somewhat irresponsible to hold someone accountable for their performance if they haven't received all the knowledge, training and resources necessary to perform a specific job or task.

Don't Assume Anything
If you aren't positive that your employees are properly trained and knowledgeable in their job duties, never make the mistake of assuming that they do. All too often, when you assume something about someone else it ends up like this; "ass / u / me." In other words, it makes an ass out of you and me!

> When in doubt, check it out.

There's an old saying, "when in doubt, check it out." This applies to just about everything in life. A person can either investigate further to obtain the necessary information or just be lazy and make some assumptions.

A thorough investigation will always provide you with the information you need to proceed confidently, whereas assuming always involves a lot of risk and is a gamble at best, often with disastrous results.

In addition to proper training and a knowledge of the job duties, everyone needs to know what the expectations and performance standards are. If you don't establish the expectations and performance standards of the job, you'll likely end up with results that vary from one person to the next. Without a clear standard of expectations and performance, the individuals performing the work are left to decide for themselves what should be accomplished.

> Establish expectations and performance standards of the job, or you'll likely end up with results that vary from one person to the next.

Leading others to self-leadership is not to abandon work standards and parameters. Rather it is the process of getting others to motivate and discipline themselves to accomplish the objectives of the job and meet (or exceed) the expectations and standards that have been established.

Chapter 11

Establish A Clear Vision
The first step in this journey begins with having a clear vision of what you want to accomplish. No, the vision is not the accomplishment of implementing this style of leadership into place. This process is the avenue which you will use to accomplish your managerial responsibilities through others.

Think of this process as a road. People drive back and forth on the road to reach their various destinations. The road is not the destination, it's the thing that facilitates traveling from here to there, or wherever it is you need to go.

Your vision should include the goals that you are trying to reach. That might seem too obvious, but I'm still surprised by organizations and individuals who have no goals and no vision. You've probably heard it said that, "any road will get you there, if you don't care where it is you're going." This is so very true of leadership.

In most successful organizations, there are usually company-wide goals and probably regional, local, departmental and team goals that you're expected to reach. Then there are the goals for yourself and your immediate subordinates. It is also important that everyone have some goals that will not only be beneficial to the organization, but to themselves as well.

> Everyone should have goals
> that benefit themselves and the organization.

I've actually known of organizations that had no goals of any substance, not even at the local level. I once heard an administrator tell his department heads that they needed to have some goals but it wasn't important that they write them down or let the administrator know what they were. A person with no committed goals is like having a clock with no hands – you can hear it ticking but it has lost its purpose.

> A person with no committed goals
> is like having a clock with no hands –
> you can hear it ticking but it has lost its purpose.

Regardless of the nature of the goal and how many of them there are, everyone needs to be aware of the goals that affect them and not lose sight of them. This is just as important for the top leader all the way down to the front line employees.

However, knowing is not necessarily doing. For example, everyone knows that you are required to stop at all stop signs, but there are many people who don't. So, how productive is it to have goals without a way to ensure they get acted upon?

Sure, you could do like most towns and cities, by having someone hand out tickets for any infractions. "Ticketing" your people might work to some degree, but would never really be effective.

Chapter 12

Effective Goal Setting
There is an entire industry regarding goals and goal setting. There are countless books, videos, tapes, lectures, pictures, posters, statuettes, and other gadgets and supplies, all with the sole purpose of helping people set and achieve goals

Because all of this information, various resources and supplies are so readily available elsewhere, I will include only an overview of this subject matter.

Direction For Desired Results
Effective goal setting is a way to provide direction for desired results that are achieved through productive application and behavior of the individuals. It involves the process of providing the direction, resources and opportunities for the benefit of others in helping them succeed.

> Helping others succeed in reaching their goals is the most important aspect of goal setting.

In many organizations if you ask people what they are supposed to be doing, you'll get a much different answer than if you ask their bosses what they're supposed to be doing. This happens all too often because there are no clearly defined goals.

It's also not uncommon to hear people say that they don't have all the tools or resources to do what they're supposed to be doing. You will also find a lot of people who haven't been given the necessary latitude or authority to do what they're supposed to be doing and are therefore being held back from success.

All too often you find people who are getting into trouble at work for not doing something that they didn't know was a part of their job or something not finished for which they don't have the tools, resources, latitude or authority to complete.

If people know what's expected of them and they have the resources to accomplish the job, they are typically much happier. It's true that happy people produce better results and higher quality. It is also true that unhappy people will produce less and what is produced will be of a lower quality.

If setting goals is such an essential part of an organization's success, then it stands to reason that helping others succeed in reaching those goals is the most important aspect of goal setting.

An effective leader knows this and knows how to use goal setting when needed and as the situation requires. Goals are usually established at the beginning of a new job, such as a new hire or someone who has recently been promoted or assigned other duties and responsibilities. Other times would include annual company-wide goals or changes in laws, rules, regulations, etc. wherein new duties, responsibilities, procedures, etc. would be assigned.

It should go without saying that all goals that are made should be done within the scope of the improvements that are desired of the person who has ownership of the goals.

Goals should be specific expectations of the future realization of behavior, knowledge, skills, and performance. They should not only be achievable, but specifically relevant to, and an integral part of each person's ongoing success.

> Goals should be specific expectations of the future realization of behavior, knowledge, skills, and performance.

Clearly Establish And Record Goals
All goals need to be specific and clearly define the responsibilities, expectations, accountability and time requirements. Both parties of the goal must clearly understand what each goal entails. Both parties should generally agree upon what needs to be done and the actions required.

Don't be overly detailed about every aspect of effort needed to accomplish the goal, just the major parts, emphasizing the main duties and responsibilities. Remember, focus more on achievements and results, and less on the mechanics of accomplishing the goals. Let your people tell you the "how" of accomplishing each goal.

Goals can be classified as either long-term (such as goals between annual performance reviews), medium-term (such as those assigned for a particular project, new job duties, etc.) or short-term (things that need to be accomplished in the next couple of days, this week, etc.).

It's not uncommon to have a variety of all these types of goals. However, and as with everything else, goals should only be made as needed and as the situation necessitates. Use goals, but don't make goals for the sake of making goals. For example, showing up to work on time doesn't require a goal. It's a given that you show up to work on time. It's also a given that you don't drink on the job, you don't steal, you don't destroy company property, etc.

> Goals are an effective tool when used properly, but lose their effectiveness when misused or trivialized.

Don't make insignificant goals, such as, "riding a bicycle to work, adjusting the thermostat or recycling paper lunch bags as a way to be conservative." While those might be worthwhile *activities*, they do not improve your people's job performance or further their success. Goals are an effective tool when used properly, but lose their effectiveness when misused or trivialized.

Goals should be recorded on paper with both parties keeping a copy. The exception to this is those goals that are simple and can easily be accomplished without writing on paper. A good example of this would be the goals for the daily shift.

Keep Goals Simply Defined
Goals should not be unnecessarily verbose or complicated. They should be as concise as possible without omitting important information. As a general rule, 300 words or less is desirable. If the goal cannot be expressed this way, you may want to consider dividing the goal into two or more goals (i.e. divide & conquer). Ensure that your people realize that the goals which have been set for them are necessary for their continued success.

> Goals should not be
> unnecessarily verbose or complicated.
> 300 words or less is desirable.

Once you have established goals with another person, it is important that the person with the goals takes ownership of the goals and is personally committed to you to accomplish them as you have agreed. Goals should never be considered as merely "good ideas" or "suggestions," but rather an essential part of each person's job duties and responsibilities.

Even though a person may have taken ownership and committed to the goals, the process does not end there. Not everyone is a super star who can work independently. All people progress at different rates and are motivated by different factors. Because of this, you will need to make goal accountability a regular part of your duties. You may be familiar with the saying, "they will only respect what you inspect."

Initially, it will be necessary to inspect your employees and their goals regularly, to see how they are progressing. This serves two purposes. First, it let's them know that you are taking an interest in their continued efforts to succeed, along with the appropriate level of accountability.

Secondly, it provides you with the opportunity to provide feedback regarding their progress and make adjustments as needed. Over time, you will know which of your employees require more inspections and which need fewer.

Unique Circumstances And Situations
There will be times where unique or special circumstances or other situations arise, necessitating new goals to address them. When this happens, make the necessary goals with your people as needed to facilitate the circumstances.

Any time you add goals, you should re-evaluate all the goals with the new goals being considered and re-prioritize the list of goals as needed.

> As a general rule, you will accomplish about three-fourths of your work through about one-fourth of your goals.

You should know that as a general rule, you will accomplish about three-fourths of your work through about one-fourth of your goals. As such, you and your people should generally focus on those goals that will yield the greatest results or "most bang for the buck." Having said that, don't neglect any important goals simply because they don't have a "big bang" right away.

Chapter 13

Ownership And Commitment
One of the most critical aspects of an effective leader is establishing ownership and commitment to whatever it is that's being done in the organization. Regardless of whether it's the company-wide goals, your goals, a new procedure being implemented, a new policy, or whatever it is, everyone needs to take ownership of their responsibilities and commit to them.

Clearly Define Expectations
It doesn't matter if it's a new hire who's just starting or someone who's been with the company for the past 20 years, the process is the same. It starts with clearly defining what it is that is being expected and the commitment they will need to make.

You've probably heard the quote, "I know that you believe you understand what you think I said, but I'm not sure you realize what you heard is not what I meant." This really underscores the importance of establishing clarification and understanding.

It is imperative to make sure the employee not only understands exactly what is required, but also any specific actions necessary for its completion. If there's any doubt whether they understand exactly what is required and necessary, it's a good idea to have them repeat back to you in their own words what they believe it is you're asking of them and that to which they will be committed.

Get Commitment And Ownership
You then need to get their personal promise and commitment to you that they will take care of the matter. The best way is to simply ask, "will you do this and can I count on you to make sure that it gets done properly?" The answer of course, should be yes. If there are any time constraints, you need to include them and make sure they commit to get the job done within the time allotted.

There is a big difference between simply telling someone they must do something and getting them to commit to it and take ownership of it. When you simply tell someone they need to do something, you have no idea what they're thinking, relative to what you want them to accomplish. You don't know if they're planning on accomplishing it or not, or when they plan on having it done.

> There is a big difference between simply telling someone they must do something and getting them to commit to it and take ownership of it.

Telling people what to do all the time leads them to feel as though you're just bossing them around. Nobody wants to be bossed around and told what to do all the time. Most people would like to have some input into how their lives are being directed.

However, when you get a commitment, the other person feels as though they have a say in the matter and they're agreeing with you to accomplish the job or task. Whether or not they actually have a real say in the work that's being done isn't what's most important.

What's most important is that they get to go through the motions of agreeing with you in the work that they're going to do. They won't feel as though you're just bossing them around. They will feel as though they're helping out and being part of the team. And ultimately, having committed team players is best for everyone.

Having a person take ownership for something, personally committing and promising you that it will get accomplished is critical. That person will be much more aware of it, making sure that it is done just as the two of you had agreed. The likelihood of it being ignored or neglected is greatly reduced, because they've given you their word or personal guarantee that it will get accomplished.

Chapter 14

<u>Involving Everyone In The Plan</u>
In order to accomplish things effectively and efficiently, everyone needs to be moving in the same direction. The direction of movement depends in large part upon the goals and objectives that you are trying to accomplish.

There may be goals that take all year long to reach, while others can be realized in a shorter period of time, even as short as a single day or shift. Whatever the goals and the direction you're headed, keep everyone focused on those goals and moving towards them.

<u>Stay Focused In Spite Of Change</u>
It is the very nature of the healthcare industry to experience constant change. Whether it's new technology, innovations, policy or procedural changes or just plain old change in census, you're going to experience a lot of change.

Without a doubt, there will be interruptions in your work flow, changes in plans, changes in the tools you use, changes in the way you conduct business. Your Priorities may shift and you may have to change directions to accommodate your business needs and demands, but don't lose focus of your goals.

Because of the inevitability of such changes, it is important to re-prioritize your work regularly to avoid being side-tracked from the big picture (i.e. the main goals and objectives). In doing so, you must effectively communicate any changes both upward and downward, to ensure that everyone is "on the same page" or "singing from the same sheet of music."

> Re-prioritize your work regularly to avoid being side-tracked from the big picture.

Communicate Effectively

While a lot of communication can be accomplished through in-services, bulletins, memos, etc., much of it needs to happen on a daily basis, shift by shift. Conducting thorough rounds at the beginning and end of every shift is absolutely essential. This allows for necessary information to flow continuously from one shift to the next, one day to the next, etc.

In addition, it is critical to communicate with your team of employees at least once during each shift. Encourage them to review and analyze both accomplishments and problems they had and what needs to be done further to accomplish the objectives.

Help them develop strategies to better manage their work. You don't have to solve their problems for them, but rather help them develop a problem solving mentality by thinking through their problems and finding workable solutions.

In most healthcare facilities, the night shift employees aren't exposed to the bulk of the management team who typically work hours that somewhat resemble "regular business hours." Therefore, it is important that each shift have at least one team leader through whom the information from the previous shifts and the management can flow to all the employees.

You will achieve a greater quantity and quality of results by helping others;
- Stay focused on goals and objectives.
- Take personal ownership and commitment to individual responsibilities.
- Become and staying more organized.
- Through clear and effective communications.
- Develop strategies to better manage their work.

Chapter 15

Providing Appropriate Feedback
Once you have established the vision (the path, goals, commitments, etc.) and opportunities for your employees to succeed, you're ready to spend less time managing and more time leading. Because you've established what good performance is and gotten commitments from your employees, it's time to observe them, to see that the behavior and results of your people match the goals and objectives you've established.

One of the key elements of being an effective leader is that you provide honest feedback to all your employees, and that they know it's honest. This is especially important for a new hire or someone who is in a new job position. People need to know how they're doing, whether it's good news or not.

Opportunities For Positive Change
There is no better way to positively effect people than providing them with feedback on their performance. Feedback, whether positive or negative provides a pivotal point from which change can occur. Positive feedback will reinforce good traits and attitudes. Negative feedback provides an immediate opportunity to evaluate, adjust and correct performance issues.

> Feedback, whether positive or negative provides a pivotal point from which change can occur.

If someone is doing a good job, they need to have that assurance that what they're doing is right, rather than worrying whether it's right or wrong and waiting to see if they get in trouble. On the other hand, someone who is doing something wrong or not up to standards should know sooner, rather than later so they have a chance to correct and improve their work.

In many organizations, people never really know whether they're doing a good or bad job unless they get into trouble. Then they learn they're doing a bad job or their work is sub-standard in some way. In extreme cases, the person never gets a second chance to make any improvements and they are simply fired.

Since most people like to know where they stand, it makes for a better work environment to provide employees with appropriate feedback. It's not as important whether it's positive or negative feedback. It's most important that it's timely and honest feedback.

> **It's important that feedback is timely and honest.**

Most issues can never be resolved unless all the facts are known in their entirety. If you are dishonest or "less than completely honest" with your people, the facts relevant to the issue will never be known in their entirety. Therefore, the issue with that person can never be completely resolved and will continue to resurface. Therefore, your feedback must be completely honest, even if it has to be brutally honest.

Timing Is Everything
It's important to provide feedback when it's due. You've probably heard the expression, "strike when the iron's hot." For the best results, whether the news is good or bad, it's important to provide the feedback when it's most effective and provides the best good. That being said, there's another saying that, "there's no time like the present." When you see that it needs to be done, it's usually best to take care of it just as soon as it's practical.

If you're genuinely concerned for the success of your employees, then being straightforward and honest with them will only help to solidify in their minds your concern for them and their success. They will know this about you and respect you for it. People who respect you will look out for your best interests and "cover your back."

> People who respect you will look out for your best interests and "cover your back."

On the other hand, most people know when you're not being honest with them and only telling them what they want to hear or putting them off. This leads to disrespect and often times outright contempt towards the person who is not totally honest with them.

People who don't respect you not only don't care about your best interests, but may even intentionally seek to undermine or sabotage your efforts. Being dishonest with people ultimately fails, usually with disastrous results. Perhaps that is why it is said that, "honesty is the best policy."

Some people have difficulty in providing honest feedback. It may be difficult or even unpleasant, especially if it's informing someone of poor performance. However, it is necessary in establishing clear and effective communications that are necessary for the other person's success (or failure).

It's important to make sure that when you're dealing with people that your efforts are sincere, with their best interests at heart. Don't try to manipulate people to get them to do anything that they're unaware of or don't agree to.

Always be straightforward and let them know what you're doing and why you're doing it (as it pertains to them). Real, long lasting results can only be brought about through changes that are genuinely motivated, not manipulated.

> Real, long lasting results
> can only be brought about through changes
> that are genuinely motivated, not manipulated.

Chapter 16

Managers Who Watch And Ding

With many organizations, their people are often the recipients of constant negative feedback from their managers. Sadly, there are many managers who spend a lot of their time trying to catch their employees doing something they shouldn't. This is especially true of new employees who aren't quite sure what to do at first. The manager keeps an eye on them and "dings" them anytime they do something wrong. Over time, they learn *what not to do,* so as to avoid being dinged.

Most employees live in fear of their bosses and try to avoid being dinged, the results of which is under-achievement. They have a fear of doing anything more than what can safely be done without being dinged, and in part because there is no incentive for them to do anything more.

> Most employees live in fear of their bosses
> and try to avoid being dinged,
> the results of which is under-achievement.

Over time, employees who live in fear settle into a mediocre routine of minimal performance and come to accept their lot in life, that they're simply an anonymous cog in the wheels of some heartless and soulless corporate machine.

On the other hand, people who are genuinely and honestly praised for their successes almost always produce at or above the organization's expectation levels. They see themselves as individuals who are contributing to the team effort and they know they are a valued asset to the organization.

The key thing to remember here is that you're praising success, not perfection. While perfection may well be the goal of any effort, there are successes along the way that need to be recognized. You'll get a lot more productivity and respect from your people if you can find genuine reasons to praise those who have earned it.

> Find genuine reasons to praise those who have earned it.

This is especially true of new people. In the beginning there may not be much in the way of success when compared with a seasoned employee, so you have to start out recognizing the small successes. You don't have to wait until they do something perfect, just doing something good or positive. Then praise them as they make bigger improvements on their way to perfection.

Positive Reinforcement
Positive reinforcement has a lot to do with confidence, which has a lot to do with a positive attitude, drive, determination and perseverance. People will naturally produce more and better results when they are appreciated for their efforts as an individual.

When you take the opportunity to praise someone;
- Be genuine and sincere.
- Make direct eye contact and tell them what it is that they did to deserve your praise.
- Smile, be enthusiastic and cheerful.
- Let them know how it helps the organization, their co-workers and the customers (i.e. patients, residents, family members, etc.).
- Tell them how good it makes you feel to see them succeeding in their efforts.
- Congratulate them and encourage them to continue with their good works in striving to reach their goals.

Praise In Public
Don't be afraid to praise people in front of others. It will magnify the effect and the feelings of accomplishment for the person being praised. Additionally, it will affect the onlookers who will want to receive the same type of praise for themselves. Allow the person being praised a brief period of time to let it soak in before you walk away.

> Don't be afraid to praise people in front of others.

After you've established an environment that encourages and rewards success, you will notice that your employees will come to you with praiseworthy accomplishments for your approval and acknowledgment. In time, they will begin to praise themselves for their successes.

Give Praise When And Where It's Due
Don't ever be afraid to hand out genuine praise to anyone who's earned it. Even the seasoned veterans of your organization need some praising to positively reinforce their contributions to the organization.

And don't be afraid to let your boss know of your praiseworthy accomplishments. Sometimes you have to toot your own horn and be your own biggest fan. However, it may be okay to be your own biggest fan, but you probably want to avoid being a "legend in your own mind!"

After having said all that, there is one caveat to this issue of praising and that is the tendency of the occasional employee to believe that simply showing up for work and doing their job is praiseworthy. In cases like this, it might be necessary to explain to them the difference between praise and a compliment or an acknowledgment for doing a good job.

In that respect, I think a compliment or acknowledgment for coming in and doing a good job is appropriate. There's a lot to be gained by letting people know on a regular basis that you appreciate all their hard work and efforts.

> There's a lot to be gained by letting people know on a regular basis that you appreciate all their hard work and efforts.

Even if it is simply showing up to work on time and doing the job they're being paid to do, you still need to routinely let them know that you appreciate their help in getting the job done. Think how much more difficult your job would be if you didn't have your people to help you!

Chapter 17

Kindness Is Not Weakness
As you implement a plan of leadership as suggested in this book, most of your employees will see it in one of two different ways. There will be those employees who see your actions as genuine, sincere and in everyone's best interests. They will appreciate you for your efforts and the opportunity for them to succeed by and through their own efforts, under your tutelage.

Then there are the employees who will see any gesture of kindness, respect or appreciation as a sign of weakness. They will not appreciate you (or others) for the positive efforts being made, but rather look for weaknesses or vulnerabilities.

Identifying Alpha Employees
Typically, employees like this will try to exploit any weakness they see in others to their own advantage. Taken to an extreme these type of people come off as being "alpha," in that they are dominant and assertive. They can even become controlling, intimidating or overbearing in their demeanor.

This type of behavior is counter-productive to effective leadership. Quite often, the alpha employee not only wants to be the "leader of the pack," but also wants to be the leader of the leader.

As such, it is extremely important to your leadership position that you are kind, yet firm. Firm isn't being mean or hateful, it's simply being unwavering in one's position.

> Firm isn't being mean or hateful,
> it's simply being unwavering in one's position.

For example, when someone comes to work late, a mean manager would likely yell and threaten the person. What ultimately happens (at least in part) is often up to the whim of the manager.

On the other hand, a manager who is firm would calmly talk to the person about being late and explain the course of action that will be taken if it continues. The outcome and what ultimately happens in this scenario is entirely up to the employee and their actions. In this instance, it has nothing to do with the whims of the manager, only the actions of the employee.

Dealing With Alpha Employees

Any alpha employee who tries to take advantage of anything they perceive to be a weakness needs to be reminded of who is the leader / manager and who is the follower / employee. This can best be accomplished by kindly, but firmly directing them back to being productive in their work.

This might go something like, "OK, <<*call them by name,*>> I really need you to get back to <<*the task or work they should be performing*>> now. I'm counting on you to get <<*the assigned task or work*>> finished by the end of the shift. You'll have that done for me, right?"

It really is that simple. If they don't go back to work and become engaged in the work and tasks assigned to them, they are being insubordinate.

Insubordination from any employee needs to be dealt with swiftly and firmly, especially with alpha employees. If allowed, even in the minutest degree, insubordination will quickly undermine your position and effectiveness as a leader within the entire organization.

A person can be reprimanded or terminated just as easily with kindness as with anger or hostility. In fact, it is always better to use kindness because any disciplinary action that is taken is not meted out from a personal level, but strictly on a business level.

Chapter 18

Identifying Performance Problems
There are several types of problems that managers and leaders come up against every day and usually several times a day. Problems ranging from manufacturing and production to office supplies and everything in between. However, this book focuses primarily on problems that deal with people and in particular how it relates to their job performance.

In the scope of job performance, a problem develops when the work or behavior that is actually happening differs from what is supposed to be happening. The greater the difference, the greater the problem. The solution to the problem is to change what is actually happening to what *should be* happening.

> A problem develops when
> the work or behavior that is actually happening
> differs from what is supposed to be happening.

I know what you're thinking, "yeah, that's sounds good in theory but how does that really happen in real life, day-to-day work?"

It's important that you realize that there is a solution to any given problem. In fact there may be many, perhaps an innumerable number of solutions to any given problem, depending upon the different variables involved. However, when dealing with job related problems, it's actually quite simple when you reduce the problem down to it's root cause.

Treating Causes, Not Symptoms
For example, in the medical field, patient treatment should be aimed at the underlying cause, not the symptoms of the problem.

If only the symptoms are treated, the problem may never go away. Symptoms are not the problem, but rather the outward manifestations of the real (root) cause of the problem. The underlying cause of any problem must be treated, which in turn will eliminate the outward symptoms.

> Symptoms are not the problem,
> but rather the outward manifestations
> of the real (root) cause of the problem.

In doing so, the first step is always to identify what is happening (the problem) that is different from what should be happening (the standard).

Then you have to ask yourself if the expectation (what should be happening) is realistic. Is it a realistic expectation of the job description? If not, then you have to change the expectation and standard so that it is commensurate with the abilities of those who are expected to perform the work.

However, if the expectation and standards are reasonable and achievable, then the deficiency lies with the person who is responsible for performing the work up to the standards established.

Once a problem is identified, you can use the divide and conquer method that was discussed previously in this book. This will help you identify the root cause of the problem and not just the symptoms.

Only after the root cause of the problem has been properly identified, should you move to the next step of resolving it, which involves reprimanding the poor performance.

Chapter 19

Reprimanding Poor Performance
The most important thing to remember about reprimands or taking corrective action is that it should provide positive result for everyone involved, including the organization. You want to correct the performance issue by eliminating the problem, without losing the person you're trying to develop. The end goal is to raise the performance in a satisfactory and beneficial way for everyone.

Positive Results Through Reprimands
Once you've identified a performance problem, you should immediately go to the person with the problem. Waiting will almost always make the problem worse in one or more ways.

Failure to reprimand when a reprimand is due, ultimately hurts the person who needs to be reprimanded. You are denying them the feedback that is necessary for them to know on a timely basis, that will ultimately affect them.

> Failure to reprimand
> when a reprimand is due, ultimately
> hurts the person who needs to be reprimanded.

If confrontation is uncomfortable for you, try to remember that you are confronting and reprimanding the *actions or behavior* of the person, and not specifically the person.

It's like the saying, "hate the sin but love the sinner." Occasionally, you'll have a deadbeat employee who just doesn't care, but for the most part, people do care. They want to do a good job and be respected for their contributions. Don't take performance problems personally, most people aren't trying to intentionally hurt you.

Being The Mechanism Of Performance

As a leader, your position should be that of being the mechanism to monitor behavior and actions, to ensure that they are consistent with the goals and standards of the organization. Taking corrective action or reprimanding someone is like the safety valve that only engages when something in the system has failed.

> As a leader, your position should be that of being the mechanism to monitor behavior and actions, to ensure that they are consistent with the goals and standards of the organization.

Remember that it is your job to try to help the person with the problem. It is their problem and you are providing the resources, assistance, direction, vision, etc. to get their performance back on track.

If you see yourself this way, you can deal more objectively and effectively with any problems that come along. However, if you take other people's performance problems personally, you're likely to deal with them personally and emotionally.

Approaching problems emotionally usually exacerbates the problem, adds additional conflict and drama, which in turn requires additional resources and effort to resolve. To be an effective leader, leave the emotions out of the problem and stick with the facts and relevant details.

When you're confronted with a problem, it's always best to deal with the specific person responsible for the problem. Never try to resolve an individual problem by involving anyone other than that particular person who has ownership of it.

You should never correct anyone for another person's mistakes, errors, problems, etc. Instead, focus on where the problem lies. Don't reprimand the entire department or group for the problems of one person. People don't like to be chided if it's not necessary and applicable to them.

Once you've established that there is a problem and a reprimand is in order, go to that person. Take them aside, away from any other people. If it's necessary to have another person witness the reprimand, include them. Never, ever reprimand someone in the presence of their peers, subordinates, customers, or anyone who isn't a necessary part of the reprimand process.

Make Decisions Based Upon Facts
Be professional and make direct eye contact. If you have first hand knowledge (i.e. you witnessed it) of the problem, tell them exactly what it is they did wrong. If you don't have first hand knowledge, tell them that you *believe* there *may be* a problem that involves them. Tell them what you believe the problem is and ask for their position.

If you don't have first hand knowledge, it's important that you don't "jump to conclusions" or accuse the person. Think of it as a courtroom setting, where they're innocent until proven guilty. Explain how the *alleged* problem involves them, and ask them how they plead (i.e. are the charges / allegations true or not) and give them the opportunity to offer evidence (i.e. tell their side of the story, provide witnesses, etc.) in their own behalf.

Don't proceed with any actions
or allegations against anyone
until you have gathered all the relevant facts.

Don't proceed with any actions or allegations against anyone until you have gathered all the relevant facts. If you have to stop and gather information from other sources, gather it immediately before proceeding with any reprimand or corrective actions.

Once you have all the facts and a reprimand is in order, tell them specifically, but briefly what it is you believe they've done wrong or what they haven't done right. Try to keep this to a minimum of a sentence or two. This establishes the problem in a nutshell.

The next step is what separates leaders from the common variety managers or supervisors. Because you are interested in developing self-leadership in your employees, you want them to be able to identify behaviors or patterns that would lead to future problems and solve them before they become problems.

Leading Others To Self-Discovery
This step is a process of self-discovery and understanding. You should ask the employee specific questions that will lead them to arrive at the same conclusion that you've reached. Not just the symptoms of the problem, but the underlying cause of the problem.

It's important that they come to the same conclusion as you on their own, acknowledge the problem, understand why it is unacceptable and take ownership of it. As such, ask as many questions as is necessary for them to come to that understanding and ownership.

Seeing, admitting, and understanding one's problems is a critical part of the development of self-leadership. Seeing the good in one's self is easy, but seeing and admitting one's problems and deficiencies is a horse of a different color.

> Seeing, admitting, and understanding
> one's problems is a critical part
> of the development of self-leadership.

However difficult or uncomfortable it may be, it is necessary for people to acknowledge their own shortcomings in order to overcome them and make improvements. To do otherwise would result in being in a constant state of denial.

This process of self-discovery and awareness of one's deficiencies is similar in practice to any variety of multi-step, self-help programs, such as Alcoholics Anonymous. For example, the alcoholic not only has to realize they have a problem, but openly admit it to themselves and others as well. Once they've overcome the denial phase and admit that they have a problem, then and only then is the person able to begin the road to recovery.

Done regularly and effectively, this process becomes less distressing in developing self-leadership skills, because it is all a part of self-improvement. When one becomes aware of, admits to, and takes ownership of any particular problem, the problem then becomes possible to overcome.

> When one becomes aware of, admits to, and takes ownership of any particular problem, the problem then becomes possible to overcome.

It's a lot like a home improvement project. In cases where significant renovations are being made, it is necessary to tear down or do demolition to undesirable parts of the house in order to rebuild those parts. When the project is completed, those parts of the home that were originally undesirable are now better, more desirable, add value, and generally improve quality of life.

Self-Induced Reprimands
When people gain an awareness through their own thought process of their problems, errors, deficiencies, etc., they will usually reprimand themselves internally more effectively than any verbal

reprimand from you ever could.

Most people see criticism, whether constructive or otherwise, as an attack on them personally and put up mental barriers to protect themselves. On the other hand, a self-induced reprimand happens internally where there are no barriers.

If all you ever do is point out your people's problems and criticize them for it, you'll always be their opponent. They will see you as their enemy and never really be on your side or support your vision, because they will fear you.

> If all you ever do is point out your people's problems and criticize them for it, you'll always be their opponent.

On the other hand, if you help them overcome their deficiencies, develop talents and habits that makes their job more productive and enjoyable, you'll always be their mentor and leader. They will always respect you, support your vision and get behind you, knowing that your direction is ultimately in their best interest.

Avoid Comparisons To Others
You should avoid making comparisons to the person being reprimanded and other employees. Don't use phrases like, "you should try to be more like this person or that person." Being compared to another person only creates resentments and negative feelings. Instead, compare their behavior or performance to the standards, not another person.

Standards are inanimate and intangible, whereas other people are very tangible and very real. Being compared to other people can be intimidating and threatening, even though the comparison may seem innocent to you.

Improving performance shouldn't be a contest with others as much as a contest with oneself. No two people are alike and no two people will perform equally. Something similar is not the same. The challenge is to get everyone constantly striving within *themselves* to want better, to do better, to be better and performing to the best of *their* abilities, not someone else's abilities.

> Improving performance shouldn't be a contest with others as much as a contest with oneself.

Don't Muddy The Water
Another important aspect of confronting people and reprimanding is to not let the facts get obscured by irrelevant information or matters. Don't allow the immediate problem to involve anything but the relevant facts. If the problem involves other factors, then by all means include them.

It's important that people know that their problem belongs to them and is not the result of some other irrelevant factors or circumstances. They have to take the blame when blame is due, just like taking credit or praising when it's due.

Once you've established a mutual understanding of the problem and the cause of the problem, tell them exactly how this problem affects other aspects of the organization. Again, don't take it personal and get emotional if the problem isn't meant as a personal attack on you. Explain how the problem affects them, their peers, the group / department, the organization, the customers, etc. and why the problem is unacceptable.

Once you've made your case, be quiet and don't speak for several seconds. Take some time for the message to sink in. In order for the reprimand to be effective, the person needs to feel uncomfortable and hopefully, remorseful for their problem.

> In order for the reprimand to be effective,
> the person needs to feel uncomfortable
> and hopefully, remorseful for their problem.

The experience should be unpleasant enough so that it makes an impression upon them so that they don't want to repeat the experience. It should provide the catalyst or turning point for any changes that may be necessary. However, it shouldn't be so unpleasant that they're traumatized by it.

Chapter 20

Proper Aptitude And Attitude Are Essential
Previously, I said that dealing with job related problems is actually quite simple when you reduce the problem down to it's root cause. At this point in the reprimand process, the problem should have clearly been identified and the person being reprimanded should have come to the realization of what actions (or lack thereof) led to the problem and knows that it is unacceptable.

Can They Do The Job?
Here's where the simplicity of this comes in. It starts by asking two very simple questions. The first question is that of *aptitude*. Does this person meet the requirements, have the know-how and skills to do the job? The question is, "can they do the job?" The answer is very simply, yes or no.

PLEASE NOTE: There may be instances where you have to consider this question in a broader sense. For example, a person with a legally defined disability, under the Americans With Disabilities Act, etc. In which case the question would be, "can they do the job with the legally required accommodations?" Be sure to stay within the confines of all applicable laws, rules and regulations in your particular area.

If the person can't do the job (with any legally required accommodations, if applicable) then they have to be removed from it as soon as it is possible and practical. Whether they can be re-trained for it and resume at a later date is another matter altogether. The main thing is right now, at this very moment, if they can't do the job, they need to be removed from it ASAP. At this point, it's not necessary to ask the second question, because it's a moot point.

Will They Do The Job?
If the answer is affirmative that yes, they can do the job (i.e. they're capable and qualified for the work), then it's time to move on to the

second question.

The second question is that of *attitude*. Is this person willing to do the job to the standards that the job requires. It's not will they kind of do the job or do it most of the time. Instead, will they do the job, the whole job and nothing but the job, in all that it entails, all of the time. The question is, "will they do the job?" Again, the answer is simply, yes or no.

If the answer is no, then the person needs to be removed from the job. How soon they need to be removed depends upon your comfort level with them and the potential for a catastrophic problem that could result by not removing them immediately.

However, it's important to remember that once you become aware of a problem, it is incumbent upon you to <u>make a plan to either correct or eliminate the problem</u>. If the answer is yes they can do the job, then you will move on to and proceed with the remainder of the reprimand process.

These aptitude and attitude questions are very key for the person being reprimanded. It takes all the guess work, uncertainty and wiggle room out of this person's future work. Either they can or they can't, either they will or they won't. It really is that simple and basic. It makes all of the "this, that and the other" excuses become inconsequential.

> Either they can or they can't,
> either they will or they won't,
> it really is that simple and basic.

Remember, don't let the issue become obscured with irrelevant information. At this point, anything other than these two simple "yes or no" questions and answers is irrelevant.

Chapter 21

The Two "Can't" Rules
This brings me to the final rule of performance issues, and why it's not all that difficult to resolve them once you get down to the basics. To be an effective manager of human resources, there are two "can't" rules that are essential for sustained success. They are simply; if you *can't* do the job, you *can't* stay.

> Ultimately, if you *can't* do the job, you *can't* stay.

That may seem a bit harsh at first, but it's a basic tenet of business that everyone should know if they are going to be employed. This is true of any "for profit" business, such as a widget manufacturer. It is even more critical in the healthcare industry, because people's health and even their lives are dependent upon the employees performing their job duties properly and on a timely basis.

Think about it, if it was you or your loved one, would you want someone overseeing your health or the health of your loved one, who was incapable or unwilling to perform all the requirements and protocols all of the time and on time?

Another aspect that needs to be considered is that of liability. Keeping people on your team who can't or won't do their job is an accident just waiting to happen. In today's litigious world, it's never beneficial for you or the organization.

It all boils down to the people who have responsibility for doing their jobs. It's not a matter of who you like or don't like. It's not about who needs the job to put food on the table for their children. It's about doing what's best and what has to be done. An effective leader not only does things right, but does the right thing.

> **An effective leader not only does things right, but does the right thing.**

Once people fully understand what the requirements and standards are, along with the repercussions of failure, it's really up to the individuals to apply themselves and exert the required effort or not.

Providing Resources Needed To Succeed
The most important aspect of this principle is that you provide the resources and opportunity for people to be successful in your organization. You work with them, coach them, provide them with all the resources at your disposal needed to be successful and then it's really up to them as to whether they will take advantage of the opportunity to have that success for themselves or not.

As I said previously, you have to think of yourself as the mechanism to monitor behavior and actions, to ensure that they are consistent with the goals and objectives of the organization. Whether people succeed or not is really up to them. However, in healthcare, the stakes are much higher than making widgets.

If people take advantage of the opportunities, then it's your job to assist them in becoming and remaining successful. Conversely, if they don't take advantage of the opportunities, then it's your job to remove them from the organization and replace them with people who want to enjoy being successful along with you.

Choices And Consequences
In this way, you never have to be the bad guy who instigates reprimands or ultimately terminates people. People bring those actions upon themselves. You're simply the mechanism to facilitate the consequences that their choices have warranted. Your responsibility is to mete out the fruits of their labors – whether good or bad depends on each individual.

As was previously discussed, the first part of the reprimand process is all about leading the person to a clear understanding and conclusion in their own minds of the problem (the difference between what's happening and what should be happening). Through this process, the person should feel bad about what they've done (or failed to do) and want to correct the problem themselves.

> People ultimately bring
> disciplinary actions upon themselves.

Getting Past The Problem
The second part of the reprimand process is all about getting past the problem, restoring the person's confidence in themselves, focusing on doing what's right and securing ownership and commitment going forward.

Throughout this discussion we will assume that the person being reprimanded is someone who you want to keep within your organization. If you're dealing with a person who clearly needs to be replaced, that's another situation altogether and will be addressed later in this book (in Chapter 26).

Whenever possible, the person doing the reprimand should be the employee's immediate supervisor and not someone with a higher position in the organization, although it would be proper for them to witness the reprimand. This ensures that the employee is responsible and accountable to their immediate supervisor, maintaining order within the group and preserving the integrity of the chain of command within the managerial hierarchy.

Reprimand The Behavior, Not The Person
It's important that the person being reprimanded realizes and understands that you are only reprimanding their actions or

behavior, not them personally.

With the same concern for them and their continued success, make direct eye contact. Let them know in plain language how you feel about their competency and performance in general (outside of this problem). Let them know that as long as there is not a repeat of the problem, the issue is behind them and you.

> It's important that the person being reprimanded realizes and understands that you are only reprimanding their actions or behavior, not them personally.

Make sure they understand that the problem is a performance related issue and that you are genuinely concerned about them and their continued success within the organization. Let them know how much you are looking forward to seeing them succeed. Tell them the next time you visit will hopefully be under better circumstances.

Once you have finished with the reprimand, let it be over. Unless the problem isn't immediately resolved satisfactorily or the same problem resurfaces at a later time, it's over. Don't dredge it back up at a later time or allow anyone else to dredge it up. Of course, you may never forget it and that's okay just as long as it stays in the past, unless it happens again.

Document Disciplinary Actions
There are various levels of severity when it comes to dealing with problems and reprimands. It is almost always a good idea to document each reprimand and keep them in the individual employee's files for future reference. It is especially beneficial to have previous reprimands for repeat offenses.

The purpose of reprimands is to identify problems and correct them so they don't reoccur. If the same problem reoccurs, then it hasn't been properly resolved and an undesirable pattern is being established.

> The purpose of reprimands
> is to identify problems
> and correct them so they don't reoccur.

For repeat problems, it is important to inform the person being reprimanded that the undesirable pattern of behavior or performance will not be allowed to continue. It must also be clearly established at what point their separation from employment will occur, should the problem continue.

Documenting a reprimand or corrective action report is the same process as the verbal process outlined above. Make sure that you date the reprimand, that it clearly identifies the problem and the course of action that is required to correct the problem and to prevent it from reoccurring. Have the person sign the reprimand as evidence that they have received it and acknowledge the requirements on their part.

Sometimes it's a good idea to include goals as part of the reprimand process. While you want to eliminate the problem, it may also be desirable to get the person to step it up a notch or two and strive to do a little bit better.

When you've completed the reprimand on paper, make sure that both you and the person being reprimanded get a copy. This provides them with a permanent record of what action on their part is required and what your expectations are for the future where they are concerned.

Have A Witness
In today's litigious world, I would suggest that when possible, another person (someone superior in job classification to the person being reprimanded) should accompany you and witness all private (i.e. where others can't see / hear you) reprimands. This is especially true where the person being reprimanded is of the opposite gender. The old saying, "better safe than sorry" applies more in today's world than ever before.

> **Have a witness accompany you in all your private reprimands.**

A successful reprimand will always include the same elements, which ultimately leads to improved self-leadership, behavior and performance. They include;
- Leading the person to an understanding of the problem.
- Allowing them to feel sorrow or regret for the problem.
- Telling them how the problem affects the people around them, the team, the organization, the customers, etc.
- Focuses on eliminating the problem and improving the person and their performance.
- Recognizing the value and worth of the person.
- Reinforcing your commitment to them to provide the resources and environment necessary to succeed.

Value And Worth
It should be pointed out here that the value and worth of a person are two different things. The value of a person can be measured in terms of what can they produce in a given amount of time.

The worth of a person is in their potential and what they can become in terms of personal growth and achievement. For example, an apple seed has value, but it is the mature apple tree as a whole that has worth.

Ultimately, a person with self-discipline who is a self-leader, will have a greater value and worth. They will consistently produce more results of a higher quality while adding intrinsic value to the team, group, department, organization, etc.

> The worth of a person is
> in their potential and what they can become
> in terms of personal growth and achievement.

For the most part, we humans are social creatures. We all have a desire, and in many ways, a need to be accepted. We want to be around other people who care about us and accept us, people who value us and recognize our worth, not only by what we are capable of giving, but as individuals who contribute to the betterment of the group, and in a larger sense, society in general.

Many people gravitate to healthcare careers where they are constantly needed and appreciated, who excel in those careers as a result. An effective leader recognizes this and benefits from helping individuals in the realization of those wants and needs in an environment that fosters self-discipline, self-improvement, and self-leadership.

76

Chapter 22

Being Fair And Consistent
Fair - *adj* - free from favoritism or self-interest or bias or deception; conforming with established standards or rules; not excessive or extreme.

Most people don't expect to get preferential treatment in the workplace, but they do want to be treated fairly. If someone has earned something, it should be given them. If they deserve something, it should be given them. Everyone wants and expects that the way they are treated in their job will be fair and consistent.

> Everyone wants and expects
> that the way they are treated in their job
> will be fair and consistent.

If the treatment of your employees in the workplace is not fair and consistent, it will have a negative effect on the overall morale. It may not be something that you can immediately "put your finger on," but it will nonetheless affect performance and impede progress.

You've probably heard that, "the only thing that is constant in life is change." In the healthcare industry, change is virtually inevitable. Even though there will be changes in your environment and that of your employees, perhaps on very frequent basis, it is important that you remain consistent in your leadership and application of practices, policies, procedures, etc.

Consistency for leaders means being the same, all the time. No, it doesn't mean that practices, policies and procedures won't change. It means that your personality, demeanor, the way you interact with people, and your leadership style remains constant, without surprises or unexpected "gotcha's" for your people.

Keeping Your Game Face On
Effective leaders have their game faces on all the time. They don't let their problems at home or with their boss affect the way they interact with others. If one person has a problem, they don't take it out on the group. They don't have favorites and nobody is beneath the radar where job performance and standards are concerned. They apply the same rules evenly across the board, for everyone.

Effective leaders adopt the organization's policies as their own policies. They don't make exceptions for one person that they're not willing to make for every person (that's favoritism at best and discrimination at worst). They don't change policies on the fly to suit the circumstances of the day. They know that practices, policies, procedures and rules are in place for a reason, to ensure fairness and consistency. That way, everyone in the organization knows what they can expect and not be surprised or discriminated against when they come to work.

> Effective leaders adopt
> the organization's policies as their own policies.

Consistency also means that you say what you mean and mean what you say. Words spoken without the appropriate actions and follow-through are just that- words. If you don't do what you say, people will stop listening to you and lose respect for what you say. You may have heard it said that, "a promise is not a promise until it's kept." For many people, a promise not kept is more like a lie, especially if they've been promised things in that past that never materialized.

Don't make promises that you can't keep for any reason. When dealing with people, it's always better to under-promise and over-deliver than to over-promise and under-deliver. The bottom line is that you do what you say you'll do, when you say you'll do it.

> The bottom line is that you do what you say you'll do, when you say you'll do it.

Employee Benefits Are Crucial

One of the most critical areas of fairness in dealing with employees has to do with their benefits and particularly, wages. You've probably never stopped to think of it this way, but employment is basically giving up part of your life in exchange for wages and other benefits.

What a person is being paid is essentially monetizing the value and worth of that part of their life that they are committing to the organization. As such, you will have a more contented group of employees if they are receiving fair benefits and being paid a fair wage, in addition to fair and equal treatment in the other areas of their job.

> Employment is basically giving up part of your life in exchange for wages and other benefits.

There may be times where you have the opportunity to get a great employee at a wage that is lower than what would be typical for your area. There may be the tendency to believe that you've found a "great bargain" or you've really excelled in your negotiating skills and gotten the starting pay to your advantage.

However, make no mistake, people know what's fair (especially their wages) and any bargain you might have gained will be short lived, as the employee will eventually find an organization that is willing to pay them a fair price.

There are too many instances to count where an employee turned in their resignation or notice, only to have their boss offer them more money. Whether the employee chooses to accept the increase in pay and stay or not, it's still insulting to the employee. If the employee was worth that much, why weren't they being paid that much from the time they became that valuable or worthy? Always pay people according to their value and worth, because it's the right and fair thing to do.

You should never, ever take advantage of someone because of circumstances or conditions. If you're always honest and fair with others, you should be able to expect the same from them. You've heard the old saying, "what goes around, comes around." If and when the day comes around where you need help from another and you've treated them unfairly in the past, chances are good that they aren't going to have much sympathy or compassion for you.

> You should never, ever take advantage of someone because of circumstances or conditions.

Pay Reviews, Raises, And Promotions

When there are practices and procedures in place for annual, performance, promotion and other types of raises, make sure that those dates and other events connected to pay increases are of great importance to you. Why? Because they are of importance and significance to your employees and the people in their lives as well.

Quite often, the person who determines when pay changes are to take effect isn't the person who finalizes the actual raise. For example, in many organizations, a manager or supervisor will determine that an employee should be given a raise and completes some paperwork. The paperwork is then given to a clerical person for processing, which is then forwarded to another person in the payroll department. As a result, there are often several "points of failure" where the process can be stopped or delayed for some reason between the paperwork being completed and the raise showing up on the paycheck.

Because there exists several points of failure (e.g. links in a chain that could break) in almost every organization's clerical and payroll systems, it would be advantageous to communicate the process to the employees. It's not important that they know how the system works, but rather that they know to follow up with you if the raise does not show up by a specified pay date (usually indicated on the paperwork that is turned in to payroll).

If a pay raise (or any other significant event) does not go through as and when it should, you should take appropriate action immediately that will correct the problem and remedy anything that the employee might have missed out on (e.g. missed wages, benefits, etc.) due to the problem.

Whether a problem in processing a raise is avoidable or unavoidable is of no consequence – the employees should not be penalized for failures in the system. If they earned something, it should be given to them and delivered as promised, period.

> Employees should never be penalized
> for failures in the system.
> If they've earned something, it should be
> given to them and delivered as promised, period.

At times, correcting this type of problem might simply involve directing the employee to the payroll clerk. Other times may involve you taking an active part in tracking down an error somewhere in the system and making sure that it gets fixed. The main thing is that you provide the necessary assistance to your employees. Why? Because it's the right thing to do and it will create employee loyalty and dedication that money simply cannot buy.

Creating A Better Work Environment

Consistency and fairness will foster a better work environment. It will eliminate power struggles within the ranks of your employees. It will eliminate feelings of discrimination or inequality. It will help to reduce petty jealousy and non-productive competitiveness.

> Consistency and fairness will foster a better work environment.

By being fair and consistent, your employees won't have to wonder what kind of "grab bag of surprises" they will be walking into when they show up for work. Your people will know that whatever problems do arise will be handled efficiently and fairly across the board. Work will flow smoother, with fewer complaints and fewer problems. Think of it as links in a chain – continuity of success is only as strong as its weakest link.

Fairness and consistency creates a beneficial cycle of better performance, better quality, better attitudes, better communication, better morale, better services, and ultimately a better experience for the customer (i.e. patient / resident). Not only does this improve the quality of life for the manager and the employees, but it extends upward, often to the highest levels of the organization.

It goes without saying that, "bad news travels fast." Quite often, the good news travels slowly and is seldom, if ever acknowledged from the executives at the top (after all, it's your job to produce good results, right?!). Nevertheless, good news still makes the executives happy, whether openly acknowledged or not. As such, it can have a trickle-down effect that positively impacts everyone involved (see Chart H-1).

Chart H-1

Chapter 23

The Need For Champions
All throughout history, the common man, woman and child have had need of champions to fight for their cause. When the commoners were without the means necessary to obtain relief for a just and good cause, they looked for someone of greater stature (i.e. someone of greater influence, strength, abilities, etc.) to engage in their cause vicariously.

In a metaphorical sense, your employees are like the commoners of old, without the means and resources to legitimately and successfully petition and negotiate with the nobles (i.e. upper level management) and royalty (i.e. company executives) concerning their cause (i.e. employment related issues).

Championing A Cause
However, before you "take up your sword and call for your white stallion," you should consider the ramifications of your undertaking relative to your vision and goals. Whenever you champion the cause for others, you are removing the responsibility for that cause from them. As such, you should always consider both sides of the matter and determine which will provide the greatest long-term benefits for both the cause itself, as well as the individual(s).

> Whenever you champion the cause for others, you are removing the responsibility for that cause from them.

As with developing self-leadership in others, it would be logical to conclude that it would be best for employees to resolve their own conflicts and issues themselves, rather than depending upon someone else to achieve the desired results for them. If you champion too many causes, you run the risk of your people becoming dependent upon you, rather than being independent and self-leading.

Having said that, there may very well be times when the best (and perhaps the only viable) way to help your employees reach a beneficial resolution to their issues (i.e. problems, concerns, etc.) is for you to champion the cause for them.

Look Before You Leap
There are a couple of things you must remember when you decide to champion a cause. Consider the following;

> 1. There should be a legitimate conflict or reason why you would be willing to draw attention to yourself from others, which might include your superiors. A good example might be an ongoing problem with the payroll system that results in your employees not receiving their paychecks properly. This might be better pursued after the employees have exhausted their efforts in dealing directly with the payroll department.
>
> 2. There should be a reasonable likelihood of success in your efforts. The outcome will likely have repercussions, either positive or negative, based upon the people who are involved or who have knowledge of your efforts, and depending on the politics involved in or related to the cause you've undertaken.
>
> 3. You need to know your limitations. You need to anticipate the amount of time and effort it will take to champion the cause, relative to its importance. If you spend a great deal of time and effort, the importance should be significant enough to justify your involvement. If not, you may want to consider delegating the cause to someone else, more suited for the task.

Political Considerations
Also, when considering your limitations, it is important to know if there is a chance you might "step on someone's toes." Quite often, championing a cause means that you will have to expose a problem in another person's department or "on their turf." Clearly, there are political ramifications to consider when you choose to confront someone on their turf.

There are a couple of business principles that you should consider when undertaking your crusade into foreign territories where there is a possibility of a confrontation. Consider the following;

> 1. There is an old saying, "mud slung is ground lost." Simply stated, you had better have irrefutable evidence and facts that there is a legitimate cause, that it needs to be pursued and why you are the person to champion it. Simply complaining, making accusations or name calling isn't enough.

> 2. You should never get into a mud slinging contest unless you possess the resources necessary to completely bury your opponent. It doesn't matter if those resources are the truth on your side, your experience or expertise, your reputation, your position, your influence, etc., they need to be sufficient to completely bury your opponent, should it come down to that.

All in all, there are many benefits to being a champion and bringing about good. Bringing about good typically improves morale while enhancing quality and productivity. In fact, from a public relations perspective, championing legitimate causes may enhance your career in any organization. Just be sure to choose your battles wisely.

Remember to ensure that your sword is sharp (i.e. get the facts straight) and your armor doesn't have any chinks in it (i.e. your cause is good and you are the person to champion it), your stallion is strong (i.e. you can bury your opponent if necessary), giving you a reasonable expectation of success.

> Bringing about good, typically improves morale while enhancing quality and productivity.

Chapter 24

Training And Development
A large part of management and leadership has to do with the training and development of human resources (i.e. your employees). It is important that you understand this process and include it as an integral part of your leadership techniques.

I'm not talking simply about the hands on training that new hires receive or the ongoing in-services, continuing education, etc. What I'm talking about is clearly establishing with your employees who the leader is and who's doing the training and providing the direction.

Everyone has or should have clearly defined job duties, goals and realistic expectations for accomplishing all of these things (i.e. the performance standards). However, there is a tendency in some people to drop the ball or slough off their responsibilities to others. If you've ever had to finish another person's work, you'll know what I'm talking about.

What happens next is that whatever got sloughed off, now "falls on your doorstep" and becomes your responsibility, because you're ultimately responsible for your people and their performance.

> There is a tendency in some people to drop the ball or slough off their responsibilities to others.

Who's Training Who?
If you allow this to happen and you have to deal with the completion of the unfinished work of others, your people are, in effect training and *conditioning* you. You're *allowing* them to train and condition you to complete the work they don't want to be bothered with. If you allow it to continue, you will have accepted

89

and assumed responsibility for the completion of that work.

Any time you're doing the work that rightly belongs to another person who could and should be doing it, you're being the antithesis of an effective leader. Not only that, you're allowing someone else to undermine the efforts that you've put into making your operation and team successful.

People cannot be allowed to leave unfinished work for someone else to do. Anyone who is allowed to do so is really training you and anyone else who's willing to accept it, that it's okay to leave unfinished work and shirk responsibilities.

> People cannot be allowed to leave unfinished work for someone else to do.

Correcting Bad Habits
When this type of activity is taking place, there are a few ways to correct the behavior and ensure that you're the leader and not the other way around.

One effective, albeit a harsh way would be to contact the person after they've left for the day and apprise them of the work they left undone. Then (usually after they've made some lame excuse) have them return and complete their work. Typically, one episode of returning to work and finishing up is all that it takes to resolve this matter.

Another option is to have a quick accounting of the day's work, goals, objectives, etc. during the shift. It could be at the beginning, in the middle, at the end or a combination of times during the shift. The minute or two that it takes to get a report a couple of times a day will save a lot of time and frustration later.

The middle of the shift is a good time (before lunch break) because you can redirect the person's efforts if necessary to ensure that the work is accomplished by the end of the shift. At the end of the shift is another good time so that you can verify that all the work was actually completed.

Ensuring that your employees effectively transition between shifts (i.e. doing rounds with the person they're replacing or being replace by, etc.) at the beginning and end of every shift will eliminate most of the unfinished work. When it doesn't, it's generally a sign that an employee is trying to be the trainer and train someone else to accept that it's okay to leave unfinished work. When this happens you'll need to reinforce the standards with the errant employee and forbid any further wayward training efforts.

> Ensuring that your employees effectively transition between shifts will eliminate most of the unfinished work.

Chapter 25

<u>Leading By Example</u>
There's nothing worse than having a manager who has the mentality, "do as I say, not as I do." To be an effective leader, you need to be continually developing and leading other people to be able to lead themselves.

It is especially important that you set the proper example of what effective leadership is all about. It's not enough to explain the standard, you must set the standard and be the standard.

You've heard the expression, "your actions speak louder than words." This is true of people who are looking to you for guidance and direction as a standard. No matter what it is that you're doing, you're teaching everyone around you every minute of the day by your actions and words.

There are literally dozens or even hundreds of opportunities each and every day to teach a lesson, set an example, or establish a standard. You should always be asking yourself, "what am I teaching others- what are my actions really saying?"

> There are literally dozens or even hundreds of opportunities each and every day to teach a lesson, set an example, or establish a standard.

If you don't "practice what you preach," you're nothing more than a hypocrite. And nobody, not even other hypocrites like hypocrites, much less respect them.

Neglecting your leadership example will quickly lose you the respect and cooperation of your employees and over time you will become ineffective as a leader.

Chapter 26

Demotions, Reassignments, And Terminations
No matter how well you do in providing the environment and opportunity for others to reach higher levels of success, inevitably there will be those who won't make it for one reason or another. In such an environment, the achievers will continue to achieve success, while the under-achievers will stand out more than they did before.

Those people who do not reach the desirable and sustainable levels of performance are not necessarily failures, even though they would seem to qualify by definition. It may be a matter of abilities, capabilities, efforts (or lack thereof), work ethic, distractions, fears, lack of confidence, personal problems, personality conflicts, not a good fit for the team, etc.

It's never the person, but rather the person's behavior, actions and performance that causes them to be removed from their positions and their employment. However, each and every person is ultimately responsible for their own behavior, actions, and performance.

> Each and every person is ultimately responsible for their own behavior, actions, and performance.

There will be people who are incapable of reaching and sustaining minimal performance standards. There will be others who are capable of success but for some reason their performance deteriorates and is unresponsive to corrective action measures. Still others who are consistent achievers will engage in some behavior or activity that is egregious to the organization and ultimately alienates them.

Unavoidable Changes In Employment

When any of these situations occur, it may be necessary to demote, reassign or terminate an employee. The main factor to consider when contemplating the separation of an employee from their position is that of benefit. Ultimately, the weightier part of the matter has to be in favor of the team, department, organization, etc.

> The main factor to consider when contemplating the separation of an employee from their position is that of benefit.

The first issue to consider is whether or not there is an organizational policy regarding the matter. If there is, then it's simply a matter of adhering to the policy regarding the matter.

For example, an employee comes to work visibly intoxicated. Let's say that there is a policy that states that such an occurrence results in immediate termination. There should be no question about what to do, except for the mechanics of meeting with and terminating the employee and escorting them out of the building.

If there is no specific policy in place or the policy gives you some discretion regarding the subsequent consequences, then you must decide what action to take. First of all, you have to consider each of your options. Your options should include job status options as well as corrective action options.

Job Status Options

Your available job status options should include, termination, leave of absence, demotion, reassignment or no change in job status. In contemplating the most appropriate path to pursue, it may be beneficial to evaluate the pros and cons using a balance sheet.

A balance sheet is simply a sheet of paper with a horizontal line drawn across the upper part of the page and a vertical line drawn down the center of the page. List the assets (pros) on the left side of the page and the liabilities (cons) on the right side of the page. As it relates to employees, assets and liabilities can be either tangible or intangible, real or imaginary (but should be based upon reasonable probability).

Assets are those qualities that add value to the organization. They may include such things as good attitude, willingness, respectful, positive, cheerful, caring, concerned, responsible, team player, consistent, productive, high achiever, punctuality, good communication skills, good documentation, long tenure, knowledge, creativity, resourcefulness, etc.

Liabilities are any negative issue that reduces the value of the organization, poses a risk to the organization or where there is a realistic possibility or threat of something negative. They may include the opposite of everything good above. Additionally, they may include previous poor performance issues, previous reprimands / corrective actions, a reasonable likelihood of future problems or negative issues, etc.

Risk / Reward Ratio
After you've had the opportunity to review the balance sheet concerning an employee, you can assign a realistic risk / reward ratio that will help you decide how best to proceed. A risk / reward ratio is simply a numeric way of looking at the employee, taking into consideration all of the real and potential risks and all of the real and potential rewards.

On the asset side of the balance sheet, assign a number from 1 to 10, where 1 is the lowest and 10 is the highest potential value of this person to the organization (i.e. the reward). Assign a number for the liability side of the balance sheet where 1 is the least and 10 is the greatest threat of damage or harm to the organization (i.e. the risk).

As stated previously, the weightier part of the matter must favor the organization. In this case, it's the ratio. A ratio with little or no risk (on the liability side) and high on the reward (asset) side is most beneficial to the organization. Anything that exceeds a very minimal amount of risk (the liability side) is probably an unnecessary risk that is usually not in the organization's best interest.

Another factor to consider is whether or not the person fits in with your organization. Are they really someone you desire in their present position or job duties? Are they representative of the organization and the image the organization desires? Do they compliment the organization's vision, goals, mission and objectives?

Once you've determined the person's value to the organization, you'll have a better idea of how to proceed with determining their job status. The decision of whether termination, leave of absence, demotion, reassignment or no change in job status is the best option should be much clearer.

> Once you've determined the person's value to the organization, you'll have a better idea of how to proceed with determining their job status.

Regardless of which course of action you pursue, make sure that you are thorough and complete with all the details of your actions. Make sure that your decisions are justified and appropriate.

There's a saying, "when in doubt, check it out." If you're unsure, check with someone who can give you proper guidance (the organization's Human Resources department, your boss, etc.). Make sure that your actions are clear, understandable, understood, and well documented.

Corrective Action Options

With the exception of termination, any other changes you make to an employee's job status should typically be accompanied by some type of corrective action, which should be documented. The corrective action should be such that it will improve future behavior and performance.

> Corrective action should be such that it will improve future behavior and performance.

Corrective action options might include suspension, probation, reprimand, re-evaluation and re-assignment of goals, etc. It is likely that the corrective action you choose will include more than one of these.

When a change in an employee's job status occurs, whether through demotion or reassignment of job position, it's important to immediately and clearly establish all the parameters of the new job. The employee needs to understand the duties, responsibilities, performance expectations, etc. and take ownership of them as with any other position in the organization.

Often, when there is a change in an employee's job status, they are assigned to a position or job that is less demanding than the previous position. Typically it means that the employee is being given one last chance to fit into the organization.

If that's the case, the employee needs to clearly understand their position and circumstances with respect to their employment. In other words, they need to know if this change is going to be their last "bite at the apple," wherein any future failure will lead to separation from employment, etc. Be specific and don't leave any room for doubt.

This is something that you would never want to lord over them in any negative way. You simply want to be honest and straightforward with them.

Ultimately it is in everyone's best interest if they succeed in their new position. You must be committed in continuing to provide them with the resources and opportunities necessary for their success, as long as it is prudent to do so.

> Ultimately it is in everyone's best interest if they succeed in their new position.

Chapter 27

Don't Be The Party Pooper

With the exception of designated events and celebrations in the workplace, work would probably never be considered to be a party. However, managers, supervisors and leaders are typically considered to be the party poopers, because they are often seen as the source of unpleasantness in the workplace.

In some ways, the traditional manager is likely to be guilty of this title. Many managers, whether intentionally or negligently hold their people back from reaching their true potential, and ultimately share in their lack of success. This includes any manager, supervisor or leader who fails to;
- Give their employees ownership of their careers.
- Provide an environment for their success.
- Provide the resources necessary for their success.
- Provide honest and regular feedback regarding their behavior and performance.

Let Go Of Control And Constraint

By holding on to traditional methods of management by control and constraint, you unavoidably hold others back and must share the responsibility of lost opportunities. You become an integral part of every employee's future, whether good or bad.

> You become an integral part of
> every employee's future, whether good or bad.

On the other hand, when you adopt and implement the management and leadership secrets presented in this book, you simply become the mechanism to facilitate the consequences resulting from the actions of others.

You can't ensure another person's success, but you can facilitate the environment and resources necessary for them to become successful. In this way, you can contribute to someone's success but never be responsible for anyone's lack of success or failure.

You'll never have to reassign, demote or terminate anyone. If you provide the opportunities for success, your employees have the choice to take advantage of it or not. Whether they take advantage of it or not, is ultimately up to them. You're simply the mechanism to facilitate the necessary consequences commensurate with their behavior and performance. Whether those consequences are good or bad is up to them.

On the other hand, the people who succeed because of the opportunities, resources, guidance, and leadership you provide them will have you to thank in part. You will have made it possible for them to be successful, leading to a better quality of life.

Success for your employees means success for you and success for the organization. It's a win-win situation for everyone.

> Success for your employees means success for you and success for the organization.

Chapter 28

To Save Or Not To Save, That Is The Question
There's a constant debate within the field of management and leadership, whether it's more beneficial and advantageous to try to salvage an under-achieving employee or replace them with someone new.

Let me start by telling a story about an employee who didn't do a particularly bad job, but never really performed up to the standards of the job.

This person's immediate supervisor didn't want to "lose the employee," believing that improvements could be made. The supervisor made all kinds of excuses as to why the employee's sub-standard performance should be allowed to continue. The supervisor assigned others to help the employee, which did nothing to improve performance. The supervisor even took time out of his own busy schedule on a frequent basis to spend with the employee, in an effort to raise the employee's performance.

Finally, after more than a year of struggling to save the employee's job, the supervisor's boss got involved and decided that more than enough time and effort had been extended to the employee. The employee was written up and given a 30-day corrective action plan, which ultimately led to the employee's separation from employment.

This may seem like an extreme circumstance, but situations like this happen more often than you might think. As we look at the factors of this extreme case, it will make analyzing and evaluating less extreme cases even easier.

Consistency In Performance Standards
The first thing that should be obvious in this case is that there was no consistency in applying the performance standards and the

obvious questions that needed to be asked; (1) can this person do the job and (2) will this person do the job?

Obviously, there needs to be a standard amount of time for any given job duties to be fully assumed by the employee responsible for those duties. For example, let's say that an inexperienced new hire should take no longer than 6 weeks to assume full responsibility of a particular job and an experienced employee should take no longer than 2 weeks to be working independently.

During the initial introductory period (i.e. when the employee first starts the job), the employee should know the job requirements, performance standards and expectation level, which would include that they are working independently within the specified time period and up to performance standards. During this time, all necessary training and other assistance must be provided to the employee that is necessary to perform said job.

A Common Mistake
A common mistake that managers make is to *assume* that everything the employee needs in order to succeed is being provided to the employee (i.e. by the person(s) assigned to do training). Therefore, they wait until the end of the introductory period before evaluating the employee's progress and performance. Quite often, the employee is not prepared to work independently and their performance is not up to standards, through no fault of their own.

> A common mistake managers make
> is to *assume* that their employees
> have everything they need to be successful.

At this point, it wouldn't be prudent to remove the employee from their position, simply because you don't really know for sure how they will perform once they have actually received all the training and resources necessary to perform the specific job duties. At this juncture, there are only two reasonable options;

1. Spend more time and resources training the employee so that you can realistically evaluate them based upon a complete and thorough training.

2. Put the employee in a productive spot, even though they haven't been properly and thoroughly trained, hoping for the best.

Neither of these options is favorable, and will end up costing you and the organization more in the long run. This is especially true if you put employees in positions for which they are not properly and thoroughly trained. It is an injustice to the employee and a disservice to the organization to do so.

Monitoring New Employee Performance

As a rule, employees should not be put into productive positions until they have received proper and thorough training AND they are sufficiently competent and proficient in their job performance.

> Don't put employees into productive positions until they have received proper & thorough training AND they are sufficiently competent & proficient in their job performance

For this reason, constant monitoring should be done on all new employees and current employees performing new assignments, job duties, positions, etc. That way, you are in a position to make changes, adjustments and tweaks as needed, early on, to ensure that each employee has had a legitimate opportunity to succeed in the job.

Once an employee has had a legitimate opportunity to succeed, it is time to evaluate them and their performance. At this point it is proper to ask the two questions; "can they do the job?" and "will they do the job?" If the answer to either question is "no," then the other part of the equation is unavoidably that they "can't stay."

Again, that may seem to be a harsh standard, but it really boils down to the kind of organization that you want to have. If you want the best of the best, you'll never reach that if you keep employees who aren't the best of the best. If you're willing to settle for less, then that's entirely up to you. When it comes to your organization, you truly will "be known by the company that you keep."

> When it comes to your organization, you truly will "be known by the company that you keep."

Getting back to our previous example, if the under-performing employee had been properly trained and evaluated early on, it would have been obvious that the two questions could not both be answered affirmatively. As a result, the employee should have been removed and replaced much, much sooner than what actually happened.

The Cost Of Keeping Under-Achievers
Another issue that needs to be considered is the cost to keep an employee who shouldn't be kept. There are several different costs associated with keeping someone who needs to go. These costs range from the obvious to the obscure, from tangible to intangible, but still costs nevertheless. Consider the following;

> 1. The most obvious cost is that of lost productivity. If the person is not performing up to standards, there is a loss between what they actually produce and what a proficient

employee could produce.

2. There is a lost opportunity cost. You have to consider what additional opportunities are or may be lost due to under-performing employees. You need to ask yourself if this is something that could prevent you from getting additional customers or additional revenue from existing customers, etc.

3. There is the potential liability cost. Any time an employee is under-performing, there is a certain amount of risk that is inherent with that sub-standard work. It depends upon the particular type of work the under-performing employee is assigned to. Obviously, an employee working in an Intensive Care Unit of a hospital has a risk factor much greater than someone who works in the housekeeping department.

4. There will likely be a morale cost. That is the cost in real terms of lost productivity from the other employees within the organization who feel that it is unfair to be asked to meet higher expectations when it is clear that others are allowed to perform at sub-standards. It is a sad reality that allowing sub-standard performance of even one employee will demoralize many others and ultimately negatively effect productivity and performance.

5. There is an intangible, but real image cost. This is the cost to your personal image, the image of your team or department and perhaps the image of the entire organization. You have to consider what effect this has or might have on your career, the organization's public relations, reputation, customer service, etc.

6. In our example, there were additional employee costs in keeping the under-achieving employee. There was the added cost of having others, including the employee's direct

supervisor, continue with an "on-going training and employee assistance plan." In other words, there were constantly at least two people who were doing the job of what one person should have been doing, for an extended period of time.

There aren't any companies that I know of who are willing to pay two people to do the job of one person, at least not knowingly. Not only that, but then there's the problem of the job of the second person being neglected. If employee "b" is helping employee "a" do their job, who's doing the job for employee "b" when they're away from their position? That's why companies hire a specific person to do a specific job.

Cutting Your Losses
Having considered all of this, there's always the question that comes to mind, "what if this person had finally come around after being *written up* (in this example, well after a year) and starts to do a better job?"

There are several factors that you could consider in evaluating this type of scenario. However, rather than have to consider this scenario, wouldn't it be best to have a system in place so that this type of scenario never happens?

> Have a system in place to provide the opportunity for success in the infancy of an employee's tenure with the organization.

If you have a system in place to provide the opportunity for success in the infancy of an employee's tenure with the organization, only successful people will ever get beyond the introductory period of employment and you'll never be faced with this kind of scenario requiring any kind of decision.

Having said that, if I were forced to make a decision in this scenario, I would choose to lose the employee even if they showed signs of improvement at the very end. Why? Because, if it takes well over a year and the assistance from multiple employees and a supervisor to raise their performance to the very minimal standard, what does that say about their future achievements?

A good rule of thumb is that, "a good indicator of future performance is past performance." Yes, it's true that people *can* and some actually *do* change for the better, but they are the exception, rather than the rule.

> A good indicator of future performance is past performance.

That's why having this system in place is so beneficial. When considering under-achievers, it's simply, "can they do the job and will they do the job?" Can they change and do better and will they change and do better?

In business, it is usually much more expensive to attract new customers than it is to keep existing customers happy and loyal. Some organizations view their employees as customers and try to provide the best possible benefits, working conditions, etc. as possible to retain employees and reduce turn-over.

Many companies have great success with this model because it elevates them above their competition. Employees naturally gravitate to organizations that visibly appreciate and reward their contributions.

However, even in this type of employment arrangement, it is the organization's best interests that must ultimately take precedence.

While an increase in employee retention and a reduction in turn-over may be desirable, there are times when turn-over is unavoidable, sometimes inevitable and at other times even desirable, depending upon the circumstances.

From my experience, keeping someone in your organization who shouldn't be there is simply "throwing good money after bad." It is counter-productive in a host of ways and is an ineffective practice at any level within the organization.

> Keeping someone in your organization who shouldn't be there is simply "throwing good money after bad."

Chapter 29

Deciding To Replace Employees
There's usually a lot of anxiety when it comes to the decision to replace someone in their job. Many managers and leaders wrestle with the unpleasant aspects of this *necessary evil*. While this may be an unpleasant aspect of the job, it's important to remember that people ultimately bring about their own consequences. If you've provided them with a realistic opportunity to succeed, they are ultimately responsible for their own success, or failure.

> If you provide employees with a realistic opportunity to succeed, they are ultimately responsible for their own success or failure.

Many organizations have specific criteria and policies involving the termination of employees. Obviously, you should conduct your employee relations within the confines of your company's policies and procedures. If you're unsure about how best to proceed, you should contact your Human Resources department for assistance. Another resource might be your immediate supervisor. In fact, in some organizations, your immediate supervisor may be the first contact you are required to make regarding terminations or other such disciplinary actions.

However, you may have an integral part in the decision making process of who to replace and when to replace them. The question then is, "when and how do you do it?" Unfortunately, there is no matrix or formula for determining that. A lot of it depends upon the circumstances, which can be simple or complex.

When To Replace Employees
Ultimately, the first step of the "when" is coming to the conclusion that an employee needs to be replaced and there is no turning back.

Next, you have to determine if the factor(s) leading to termination are such that immediate termination is necessary. If it is necessary, you have no choice and you should facilitate it as soon as is possible and practical.

If, on the other hand, immediate termination isn't required, you have to ask yourself, "what will be most beneficial to the organization (or team, department, etc.)?" Should you terminate now or try to find a replacement first? Often times it's not what's actually *best* as much as it is "the lesser of the two evils." It may come down to what is the least damaging course of action that can be taken.

> You have to ask yourself, "what will be most beneficial to the organization?"

All matters of disciplinary action and particularly terminations must be kept confidential and away from all employees other than those who are key and have a need to know. An employee who is being involuntarily replaced should never know about it until the moment it happens. The saying, "loose lips sink ships" is wisdom that will never fail you in business.

How To Replace Employees
After you've determined the "when" part, you need to consider the "how" part of replacing the employee. This can be as simple as hiring and training another employee to replace the departing employee. This can happen before or after the employee is terminated. If before, the new employee simply fills the vacancy created by the departed employee. If after, the departing employee is terminated after the new employee is ready to be productive.

I know a manager who had two employees who were very proficient and productive employees. Unfortunately their success led them to believe they were "special" and that the rules didn't really apply to them. They began drinking on the company premises after hours. They weren't necessarily "drinking on the job" because it was after normal business hours, but the company had a "zero tolerance" policy prohibiting the consumption of alcohol or drugs on company property.

The infraction of this particular company's policy did not mandate *immediate* termination, but it did require the termination of any violators. Because the employee's violation of company policies did not affect their actual on-the-job performance, the manager kept them employed and hired two new employees. The best trainers it turns out were the two employees who were to be replaced. Wanting the best training for the new employees, the manager had each departing employee train their replacement.

Once the new employees had been trained, the manager invited the departing employees into his office where they were advised that the consequences of their choices had resulted in the termination of their employment. The employees left the property, the manager posted a new work schedule and the organization continued to operate successfully.

Protecting The Organization's Interests
How you choose to replace departing employees with new employees is ultimately up to you, but should represent the best possible scenario for the organization (i.e. the various teams or departments in which the departing employees may be working, etc.) and it's continued success.

> It should be clear to everyone that
> the organization rewards success and doesn't
> tolerate bad performance or bad behavior.

113

It goes without saying that legitimate disciplinary action and particularly terminations have the effect of reinforcing the importance of respecting the organization's position and relationship to the employees. It should be clear to everyone that the organization rewards success and doesn't tolerate bad performance or bad behavior.

It should also be clear that the managers / leaders don't abuse people, but are simply the mechanism for administering the consequences that the employees ultimately choose for themselves.

> Leaders don't abuse people,
> but are simply the mechanism for administering the consequences that the employees ultimately choose for themselves.

Chapter 30

Dealing With Time Wasters
Time wasting can best be described as any unnecessary and/or unacceptable time that is spent in the workplace doing any activity that is contrary to organizational and/or personal standards, goals and objectives. The emphasis is placed on the words, *unnecessary* and *unacceptable*.

Unfortunately, in the healthcare industry, the more the job duties involve direct patient / resident care, the less time there is that could be considered discretionary.

For example, the administrator of the facility may spend leisure time with doctors, vendors, sales reps, etc. It may include having lunch or engaging in other social activities that are far removed from direct patient care. However, that is a necessary component of the administrator's job function.

On the other hand, the aides assigned to the patients / residents have virtually no discretionary time, because their time is entirely devoted to patient / resident care.

In the healthcare industry, the care givers typically have little or no discretionary time. The expectation is that all time on the job is for the express benefit of the patients / residents. Every minute of every day spent at work (with the exception of breaks, meetings, etc.) should be done with the focus of improving patient / resident care, and to some degree, their family members.

> Every minute of every day spent at work should be done with the focus of improving patient / resident care, and to some degree, their family members.

Others Who Waste Your Time

It's been said that, "the person who has all the time in the world wants to spend it with the person who can't spare a minute." People who waste their time usually waste it with others who shouldn't be wasting their time either.

Whether directly (i.e. engaging you personally) or indirectly (i.e. time expended to get employees back to productive work), your time is ultimately wasted as well.

Time wasting can either be a nuisance or a performance issue. If it's a performance issue, it simply needs to be addressed like any other problem (i.e. reprimand and/or other corrective action as may be required).

> Time wasting can either be a nuisance or a performance issue.

Sometimes the time waster is someone who is unsure of themselves and requires constant feedback. Because of their lack of confidence, they come to you constantly for reassurance or guidance.

While this type of behavior might be acceptable in a new employee or an employee in a new position, this shouldn't be allowed to continue for any length of time beyond what is reasonable for the person to perform their job duties independently. If it continues beyond a reasonable time, then it has become a performance issue and needs to be addressed.

Quite often people will come to you because they want to visit with you or take a little break from what they're doing and who better to waste time with than the boss. It's hard to get in trouble for wasting time when it's being done with the boss. They may even come to you with a legitimate concern, to which you are almost always obligated to listening and providing assistance.

Redirecting And Penalizing Time Wasters
When this type of scenario happens, the most effective thing to do is to immediately start walking to the time waster's work area. They'll have no choice but to follow you, and can talk to you along the way.

Once you get to their work area, stop and finish the conversation, but only to the extent that it's necessary, don't chit-chat. Once the conversation has ended, simply direct the employee back to their job duties. If there is a follow-up necessary, remind them that you'll get back to them.

Make sure to follow-up with your people as necessary. If there is no need to follow-up, let them know. However, if there is a reason and you specifically tell them that you will get back with them, then by all means, keep your word and follow-up as promised.

IMPORTANT: Never let time wasters waste their time in your work area. Always walk them directly back to their work area.

> Never let time wasters
> waste their time in your work area.

If you believe the employee's time wasting efforts were not legitimate (i.e. they clearly just wanted to waste your time and didn't have a legitimate issue to discuss with you), you need to provide a "deterrent" to such activities.

An effective deterrent is easily accomplished by adding additional tasks to the employee's work load that must be accomplished before the end of their shift. It need not be something that takes hours of work, but something that will take some additional time and "penalize" their time wasting actions.

Pretty soon, time wasters will learn that deviations from their work and attempts to ensnare you into time wasting activities will ultimately lead them back to their own work area and back to work. They will also learn that intentional time wasting will be rewarded with additional work, which they will likely avoid.

> Intentional time wasting should be rewarded with additional work.

This process also works well with time wasters who want to call you after hours. For example, let's say you have a night shift employee who always calls you in the middle of the night with some non-emergency question or concern that could have waited until the morning when you're up and at work yourself. As a deterrent, every time the employee calls with a non-emergency issue, simply include some additional work that must be accomplished before the end of their shift.

Non-Confrontational Redirection
For those times where you catch your employees all huddled up around the water cooler or other gathering location wasting time, you can achieve the same results by redirecting and assigning extra tasks.

For example, let's say you walk past the gathering place and find a handful of employees chit-chatting and wasting time. You say something like, "I see that you have some free time on your hands. You know what I always say, If you've got time for talking, you've got time for stocking. Therefore, I need each of you to <<*assign additional task(s)*>> before you leave today, so let's get to work on that right away."

There are a few clever poetic work-related sayings that are sure to drive the point home, especially when you assign additional tasks along with them. They are;
- If you've got time for talking, you've got time for stocking.
- If you've got time for yacking, you've got time for stacking.
- If you've got time for leaning, you've got time for cleaning.
- If you've got time for stopping, you've got time for mopping.
- If you've got time for sleeping, you've got time for sweeping.
- If you've got time for griping, you've got time for wiping.
- If you've got time for whining, you've got time for shining.

The bottom line is that time wasters will always waste time unless there is an incentive to deter them. If your policy and practice is clear that wasting time equates to additional work, time wasting will typically end rather abruptly. As with everything else, consistency is essential to long term success.

> Time wasters will always waste time
> unless there is an incentive to deter them.

As previously discussed (in Chapter 17, "Dealing With Alpha Employees"), it really is that simple. If they don't go back to work and become engaged in the work and tasks assigned to them, they are being insubordinate.

Again, insubordination from any employee needs to be dealt with swiftly and firmly. If allowed, even in the minutest degree, insubordination will quickly undermine your position and effectiveness as a leader within the entire organization.

Chapter 31

Working With PRN Employees
With the exception of fewer hours, PRN employees should have the same policies, standards, considerations, etc. as the full time employees.

If there is a likelihood of extended periods of time between days that a PRN employee will work, it may be a good idea to maintain an informational log book. The management can update the log book as necessary with any pertinent information that needs to be disseminated. This will aid in keeping all employees informed of any important information, policy and procedure changes, etc.

Working With Agency / Temp Employees
There may be times when you need to outsource your employment needs. Even though temp employees may not be employed by your organization, they are nonetheless an extension of it. As such, they should have the same policies, standards, considerations, etc. as the regular employees. When used effectively, an outsider looking in at your staff shouldn't be able to tell the difference between the temp and regular employees.

> Agency / temp employees should have the same policies, standards, considerations, etc. as the regular employees.

The agency who is providing the temps should have a thorough understanding of not only your organization's policies and procedures, but the social and political climate of your facility as well. This information must be provided (i.e. trained, in-serviced, etc.) by the agency to all temps who will be working in your facility. Any changes in your organization's policies, procedures, protocol, etc. should be communicated immediately to the agency.

This will ensure that all temps who work in your facility are up to speed with all necessary and pertinent information.

While all employees, full time or temp, should maintain the same performance standards, your approach to leadership with temps may vary. If the temp is very short-term in their employment (e.g. filling in for someone's vacation, etc.), you won't need to spend much time (if any) setting goals, sharing your vision, coaching, etc.

Consider Temps For Full Time
There are times when temps have the opportunity to transition into a full time position of employment. When you have this type of a temporary employment arrangement, you should take the time to set goals, share your vision and coach the temp as if they are going to be a full time employee. That way, you'll get to see how they perform along side your regular employees and there won't be any guessing as to whether they will fit in with your team, should the opportunity present itself to employ them.

While you may not have the authority to administer disciplinary actions directly to temps as you would with your regular employees, you can work with the temp agency as needed to facilitate appropriate behavior. If necessary, you still should have the authority to terminate a temp's activities within your organization at any time and remove them from your place of business.

> Using temps gives you the option to "try before you buy."

Pros And Cons Of Temps
As with any employment situation, there are pros and cons when working with temps. On the positive side, you often have the option to "try before you buy." You may go through several temps

before you find one that will fit in with your organization as a regular employee.

Because the temp is employed by an outside company, you don't have to deal with any employment related issues, such as payroll, benefits, worker's comp, etc. until you actually employ the person.

On the negative side, temps usually cost a higher hourly rate, which will affect your payroll, budget, etc. Quite often, if you decide to employ the temp yourself, there is usually a cost that must be paid to the temp agency. Another possibly negative aspect of temps is that you don't have as much direct influence in the relationship as you would in the typical employer / employee arrangement.

Chapter 32

Simplifying The Recruiting Process
Adding more employees typically occurs when organizational production increases, which necessitates additional manpower or when a job position becomes vacant for one reason or another.

Sometimes there is advance notice of a hiring need, such as organizational growth, retirement, resignation, reassignment, etc. Other times there is no notice, such as immediate terminations, illness, death, etc. Regardless of the circumstances, having a system in place will make the process easier and better.

> Having a system of hiring in place will make the process easier and better.

Advertising, Marketing, And Networking
Obviously, the first thing that needs to be done when trying to increase your staff is to make your intentions known. This can be accomplished through a variety of ways, including traditional advertising, such as newspapers, radio and television.

There are additional methods available through internet technology, such as local online ads and classified listings, employment web sites as well as various social and professional networks. You may wish to consider recruiters (i.e. headhunters) when filling key positions.

Perhaps one of the best methods is the good, old-fashioned practice of networking with your peers and associates. Most good employees already have jobs and aren't making an effort in looking around for openings, unless they're ready to make a change. However, most people, no matter how good they are, are always open to *opportunity*. It may be someone you know, or someone who knows someone else who may be interested in the opportunity that you offer.

Fishing For Results
There is a principle of advertising and marketing that says, "you should fish *when and where* the fish are biting." That being the case, you should take advantage of every marketing and advertising avenue available to you that is applicable to your situation.

For example, don't advertise for a Neurosurgeon in the local nickel paper or use a professional recruiter to fill a housekeeping position. But do learn of and take advantage of all avenues available, especially since many of them don't cost anything more than a little effort.

Keep in mind that the first impression people will get of you and your organization will be from their initial exposure. There's a dandruff shampoo commercial that reminds us that we never get a second chance to make a good first impression. Some of the people you are trying to attract to your organization and ultimately to you may have no knowledge of you or your organization.

Therefore, you want your advertising and marketing to be a reflection of who you are and the image you are trying to project to the public. Image is everything, especially when you are competing against others for the same prospective employees. If you don't have the best offer amongst your competitors, you'll end up with the left-over job seekers who didn't get hired as they worked their way from the top of their list down to you.

> Image is everything,
> especially when you are competing against others
> for the same prospective employees.

Cost Effective Advertising

At some level, cost has to be considered as a factor. Obviously it doesn't make sense to take out a full page ad in the newspaper, when a single column, 5-line ad will do the trick. However, the more important the position is that you're trying to fill, the more critical it is to effectively advertise. More often than not, "you get what you pay for."

With the internet being such an integral part of our daily lives, there's almost no excuse not to have an internet presence that showcases your organization. A professionally designed web site provides marketing and advertising 24 hours a day, 7 days a week, 365 days of the year, at a negligible cost.

If you have a professional web site, include it in your your other marketing and advertising. You can present an almost limitless amount of information on a web site that can be more effective and more affordable than any other form of media.

The one thing that you must never do is over-sell your organization or promise more than you can deliver. Not only will you be wasting your advertising dollars, you'll be wasting your time and the time of prospective employees.

> The one thing that you must never do
> is over-sell your organization
> or promise more than you can deliver.

Be honest and accurate with your advertising and choose your words carefully. If there is going to be any discrepancies between what you advertise and what you actually have, it's best if you under-sell and over-deliver, rather than vice-versa.

If it makes it easier, think about how you would feel if you were looking for work and answered an ad that was not as it appeared to be, especially if it was misleading. How valuable would your time be as a prospective employee and how would somebody wasting it make you feel?

Accepting Applications
Once you've got your advertising, marketing and networking working for you, you've got to make it easy for prospective employees to make the initial contact to "put their name in the hat." If the only way you have for people to apply is in-person, you'll be missing out on people who might just be who you're looking for.

When possible, it is ideal to have an internet presence where prospective employees can complete an application and submit it online. In the absence of a online application, there should be a way for an applicant to download an application that can be emailed, faxed, mailed or dropped off.

Email is an effective way for someone to send a resume or scanned application. A resume is usually sufficient to determine whether or not you want the person to come in for an interview, at which time they can complete a formal application.

Your ad should also include an email address and fax number where a resume can be submitted, as well as a contact telephone number where an applicant may call for additional information.

Make it easy for job seekers
to get their names into your hat!

Chapter 33

Conducting Effective Interviews
The next step is to review each application or resume and sort them into two piles- interested and not interested. Contact each applicant you're interested in and arrange for a personal interview.

You should schedule interviews far enough apart so that you don't have someone waiting for any length of time while you're finishing the previous interview. Poor time management and a casualness to the importance of their time may come across negatively with the applicant. Set the example and remember, your actions speak louder than words and this will likely be their first impression of you and the organization.

> Set the example and remember,
> your actions speak louder than words.

Using An Interview Checklist
In successful business, having reliable systems and procedures ensures quality and consistency. Having a system for interviewing should be no different. Consider the following checklist to assist you in preparing for your interviews;

> 1. Know who you're interviewing – remember the name of the person you'll be interviewing. When you eventually meet them, make eye contact, shake their hand firmly and calling them by name, thank them for coming in to meet with you.

> 2. Probe the job application prior to the interview. Identify and highlight any questionable items, uncertainties, discrepancies or things that don't add up or make sense. Make notes on the resume or application to clarify any

concerns you may have.

3. Make notes of the questions you intend to ask so that you don't forget. You may find it beneficial to use a template or organized list from which to draw your questions (see Appendix A).

4. If the applicant has to wait for any reason, try to provide a comfortable location for them while they are waiting. This location should include some printed information about the organization, such as pamphlets, newsletters, etc. If applicable, it should also include any industry related magazines, periodicals, etc. At the very least, there should be some type of interesting reading materials for them to read while they wait. It would be courteous to offer them a glass of water or something to drink while they wait. Let them know where the rest rooms are in the event there is a need.

5. Choose a location for the interview that provides an informal setting, such as around a table, in a meeting room, etc. Try to avoid a formal environment that creates a "boss / employee" setting, such as sitting across a desk from the applicant. You want the applicant to open up to you, which is less likely in a formal setting and more likely in a setting that is casual and relaxed.

The Two Parts Of An Interview

An effective interview consists of two basic parts. The first part of the interview will be the "extraction phase," in which you will try to extract relevant information from the applicant. This phase consists primarily of you questioning the applicant. Part of this process also involves the applicant trying to sell themselves to you, such as showcasing their talents, accomplishments, etc.

The second part of the interview process will be the "infusion phase." This is where you will provide information about yourself, your team, your department, the organization, etc. This phase will probably be a mixture of you providing details and allowing the applicant to question you. If you desire to employ the applicant, this is where you will try to sell yourself and the organization to them.

Focus On Critical Factors
The saying, "an ounce of prevention is worth a pound of cure" is applicable here. The *ounce* of time you spend up front to thoroughly screen out potential "bad hires" will be much better spent than the *pound* of time (not to mention the frustration) that will almost certainly be required to address problems later as a result of bad hiring. This is especially true if you take into consideration the frustration and other associated problems (e.g. sub-standard performance, morale issues, etc.), that often accompany bad hires.

Critical factors are just that, factors (i.e. characteristics, traits, behaviors, etc.) that you consider critical in employees who work for you and your organization (see Appendix A). There are many factors to consider, but it is ultimately up to you to decide which are the most critical for you when considering applicants.

> It is ultimately up to you to decide which factors are the most critical for you.

There are basic factors that should be considered for every employee at any position. There are still others that should be considered for key (i.e. supervisory, managerial, leadership, etc.) positions. There may be other occasions or circumstances which necessitate adding additional factors to the list provided here.

For example, such additional factors might include issues relating to substance use & abuse, legal & criminal, financial & credit, personal grooming & hygiene, health & fitness, etc., depending upon the nature of your needs.

Having said that, it is also important that you don't have critical factors that would be considered discriminatory or illegal in nature.

The factors you determine to be critical to you, should be representative of where your organization is or where you want it to be, regardless of where it is now. If you don't like where you are now, work towards becoming what you desire to be. This is true in all of your actions and activities, whether hiring new employees or working with current employees. Remember, "if you always do what you always did, you'll always get what you always got."

> If you always do what you always did,
> you'll always get what you always got.

When considering these critical factors and using them as a measuring stick, you will be able to better gauge how well any given applicant will fit in with your organization. You'll also have a better idea of whether or not they will add value to the organization, and if so, how much value you can or should be able to legitimately expect.

The Mechanics of Interviewing
The basic premise of the interview is that you want to hire the right person for the job and the applicant wants to obtain what they would consider a "good job." The upside for you is filling a vacancy that may be adversely affecting your team or organization.

The downside is the risk of hiring people who aren't the right fit for the organization and your existing team. This could end up costing you more in the long run, and not just money, but time, effort, emotion, morale, continuity of care, etc. Bad hires are never beneficial for either party.

The interview is an opportunity for each party to benefit. The applicant gets to showcase his or her talents and propose how your team and the organization can benefit from them being hired. You get to consider critical factors of the applicant in evaluating any benefits that can be derived from hiring the applicant.

There is a distinct opportunity for either party to provide misinformation. The applicant may exaggerate or even lie about critical factors in order to get the job, especially if they are desperate for employment. The interviewer may be tempted to exaggerate the benefits of the job, or be deceptive about the job duties, requirements, performance standards, etc., especially if they are desperate to hire.

Digging For Information
It is your goal to ask enough of the right kinds of questions to ferret out the potential value of the applicant being interviewed. The right kinds of questions will help you distinguish fact from fiction. It may be a mistake to casually accept everything they say as absolute truth.

> The right kinds of questions will help you distinguish fact from fiction.

Most people see themselves differently than the people who are, have or will supervise them. And even if they don't, everyone knows that you present the very best of yourself in an interview. You must look past any facade to get the details you need to make an informed hiring decision.

Don't let appearances be deceiving. It is true that you can't judge a book by its cover. You should spend enough time with the applicant to learn not only what's on the cover, but what's really in the pages underneath, whether it's good or bad.

Don't confuse nervousness with deceit. If a person is nervous, they may come across awkwardly. However, nervous or not, their answers and demeanor should still be consistent.

On the other hand, being too confident and cocky may also be an indicator of deceit or other potential problems. The more you can help the applicant relax and see who they really are, the easier it will be for you to see their potential value.

During The Interview
It's a good practice to make and maintain eye contact as much as possible. If the applicant constantly avoids eye contact or seems uncomfortable with certain questions, it may be a signal that they're trying to hide something. If you have any uneasiness or uncertainties about their answers, continue to explore with additional questions until you are satisfied one way or the other.

Whenever possible, you should avoid yes/no questions unless there's no other way to get the information. Yes/no questions rarely, if ever reveal anything. Instead, use open-ended questions as much as possible to get and keep the applicant talking about themselves, their experience, skills, etc. Use questions that include; "tell me," "what," "how" and sparingly use "when," "where" and "which" and try to avoid "why" questions altogether.

> Use open-ended questions as much as possible to get and keep the applicant talking about themselves, their experience, skills, etc.

Asking "why" questions tends to put people on the defensive. "Why" questions typically require having to justify something, such as an action or behavior. For example, "why did you do that?" or "why didn't you do this?" Instead, follow up with exploratory questions, such as, "how did that turn out?" or "what results did that produce?" or "if you had it to do over again, is there anything you would have done differently- explain."

Think about how your questions will make the applicant feel. Your objective is to encourage them to open up and tell you about themselves. You want to understand them better to see if they will fit in with your team. Pressure causes people to be reserved, anxious and defensive, while being casual and relaxed allows them to relax and open up.

Ask The Right Questions

A practice of good interviewing is to avoid leading questions. Leading questions are just what the name implies, questions that begin by leading the applicant in the direction of where you want the answer you're looking for to go. You're not the director of a movie who prompts the actors with their cues and lines, so don't direct the applicant to the answers you're looking for.

You should be more like a police detective trying to find the facts necessary to solve the case. Remember to be the "good cop," you know, the one who pretends to be looking out for the best interests of the crook. Never be the "bad cop" who's mean, tough, threatening and overbearing.

Make sure that you let the applicant do 90% of the talking during the interview. Don't be over zealous in promoting the benefits of the job until after you've concluded that the applicant may fit in with your team.

> Make sure that you let the applicant do 90% of the talking during the interview.

The most important thing for you is to gather enough information needed to make a good hiring decision. The only way for that to happen is to let the applicant provide that information to you.

Don't Be Naive
Be sure to clarify any questionable items, uncertainties and discrepancies (if any) that were previously highlighted in the job application or resume. If anything stuck out to you as you reviewed their application or resume, make sure you address those issues. It may be something as simple as an unexplained gap in their employment history. Whatever it is that makes you wonder, find out during the interview, not later.

Verify any grandiose claims, whether they're made in the application, resume or during the interview. Ask the applicant to substantiate any such claims. Encourage them to be specific and provide details.

Another interviewing technique is to use hypothetical situation questions. This lets you see how applicants think on their feet and how they would react to problems or situations that could arise unexpectedly in the workplace. You may want to consider using details of an actual event from the past that will be important to know how they would react. Be specific with the details of the situation so that you can accurately gauge the quality and relevance of the answer given.

> Use hypothetical situation questions to see how well applicants can "think on their feet."

After The Interview
If you feel that the applicant will not fit in with your organization, don't spend a lot of extra time with them. Thank them for coming in to visit with you. Tell them that you will be reviewing their

application with your management team and if you decide to make them a job offer, you will call them back. Don't promise anything and politely show them out.

At the end of your questions, you should have at least a gut feeling as to whether or not the applicant may be a serious contender for the job. If so, you want to have the opportunity to sell them on the organization and yourself. Take some time and let the applicant ask you questions. Their questions can be as important as their answers. Questions asked by applicants can be very revealing about themselves.

> Questions asked by applicants can be very revealing about themselves.

If you're interested in employing the applicant, spend a few minutes highlighting your team and the organization. Tell about your own positive and successful experience with the organization and how it has benefited you in your position / career and adds to your quality of life, etc. Accentuate the positive aspects of the organization, which could include the caring management staff, the quality of the team, the teamwork environment and any other extras that might add to their enjoyment and quality of life as a member of your team.

Briefly explain the goals and objectives of the organization and management staff A more thorough explanation and vision can be given in orientation and/or training. Cover the expectations and performance standards required for the position.

Explain pay rates, pay dates, and all other benefits that are offered to the applicant. Let them know if there are any waiting periods or probationary periods that must be met to begin receiving benefits. Thoroughly cover any prerequisites of the job, which may include drug test, credit check, background check, etc.

Don't Promise Anything Just Yet
It is important that you do not promise the applicant anything until the formal offer of employment is made. If there will be more than one interview, the offer of employment and other details shouldn't be clarified and finalized until after the final interview.

It is often favorable to have a second interview with another member of the organization. If the position being filled is a key position, it may require more than two interviews. Having a second person interview the applicant may uncover additional information that is critical. You know the old saying, "two heads are better than one."

> A second person interviewing the applicant may uncover additional information that is critical.

If time is of the essence, you may want to conduct the second interview immediately after the first. If so, tell the applicant that you want another member of the management team to spend a few minutes with them. Ask them if that would be okay. Then step away and briefly review the applicant with the second interviewer, specifically in regards to any concerns, reservations about them, etc. where the second interviewer should probe further or clarify any issues or concerns.

If the second interview will be happening at another time, schedule a mutually convenient time for the interviewer and the applicant. Thank them for coming in and let them know that you are looking forward to seeing them again.

The Second Interview
As with the first interview, the second interviewer should try to be

comfortable and relaxed with the applicant.

If the first interviewer has any concerns and/or reservations, the second interviewer needs to ask additional probing (preferably open-ended) questions. This will allow the applicant to explain and/or clarify the concerns one way or the other.

The second interviewer doesn't need to ask the same questions as the first interviewer. The purpose of the second interview is to either confirm or dispel the first interviewer's impressions of the applicant.

The second interviewer should ask enough questions and extract enough information to assist in the final decision making process. Additionally, the second interviewer should allow the applicant to ask any questions they may have and clarify any of their concerns.

> The purpose of the second interview
> is to either confirm or dispel
> the first interviewer's impressions.

If you're not absolutely sure you want to hire the applicant, let them know that you will be reviewing other applications and if you decide you want to make them a job offer, you will call them back by a certain date. Tell them that if you have not contacted them by that date, you won't be making them an offer. Thank them for taking the time to come in to visit with you. Don't promise anything.

Choose Your Words Carefully
Do not say or do anything that would prevent the applicant from applying at a later date. Most organizations are Equal Employment Opportunity Companies and you don't want to violate any laws or cast your organization in a bad light.

Whatever you do, don't give anyone any unreasonable or false hope, lead them into believing there's something when there isn't or leave them hanging. It's always best to be up front and honest with people.

Remember, interviewing is just like any other part of business, in that it works best when you have a plan and a system to achieve success. Don't be haphazard, sloppy, or hurried when interviewing. Take your time and make sure to *extract* and *infuse* the necessary information for both parties to make an informed decision.

> Don't be haphazard, sloppy, or hurried when interviewing- take your time.

Making The Employment Offer

Once you have made your decision to hire, proceed with the offer, subject to completion and finalization of any prerequisites. Before the actual offer is made, you may wish to consider giving the applicant a tour of the facility, introduce them to some team members, show them where they will be working, etc. Some companies have applicants spend some time (a few hours to an entire shift) observing the workplace or volunteering before finalizing the offer.

Once all of the hiring prerequisites have been met, it's time for you to formally make the offer to the applicant. It's always best to make the offer in person whenever possible, rather than over the phone, via email, etc. It gives you one last look at the person as an applicant rather than an employee. If you have any additional questions or reservations, you can address them before they become your employee.

If the issue of pay hasn't already been agreed upon, finalize it before you proceed. Remember, you're not trying to get a bargain, but rather establish a fair and reasonable value in exchange for the applicant's time they will spend working with you.

Before making the offer, it is imperative that you start each applicant off with the ownership and commitment that they will be expected to assume during their tenure on your team. Review the job duties, requirement, performance standards, goals and objectives.

> Start each applicant off with the ownership and commitment that they will be expected to assume during their tenure on your team.

Get them to personally promise to you that they will in fact do what is required. Again, the best way is to simply ask, "will you do this and can I count on you to make sure that it gets done properly?" The answer of course, should be yes.

Once you've gotten their promise of ownership and commitment, proceed with the offer. Try to be professional and avoid the "you just won the lottery, jump up and down" offer. Instead, review with them how their qualifications, experience, expertise, etc. will fit with your team. Let them know that you're looking forward to their contributions in achieving not only their own personal success, but the overall success of the team / organization as well.

Ask the applicant if they have any unresolved questions or concerns that need to be addressed. Once all questions and concerns have been resolved, make the official offer of employment. I see it going something like this, "<<*call them by name,*>> I'd really like to have you on our team and if you'd like to be a part of it, let's get you going. When can you start?"

After the applicant accepts your offer, finalize any details and establish a work schedule. Also, it might be a good idea to introduce them to some of the other employees, supervisors, etc. Make sure that they meet the person who will be training and mentoring them. Before they leave, make sure that you shake their hand and welcome them aboard.

Prerequisites To Hiring
If there are any prerequisites of the job (e.g. drug test, credit check, reference check, background check, etc.), explain the process in detail. Make sure there are no misunderstandings, what is required and the process involved. Be sure to supply the applicant with any forms, paperwork, materials, etc. as needed Make sure they understand any time deadlines, constraints, etc. for the completion of the process.

It may be a good idea to have them call you back in the minimum number of days it takes for the any prerequisite processes. In other words, if it takes 4 business days to get the results back, instruct and commit the applicant to contact you directly (i.e. don't leave a message) after 4 business days.

You might want to set a reminder on your calendar (that you check every day) when the applicant's information should be completed. Follow up and get the information ASAP, so that the hiring can proceed if possible.

> The last thing you want is for one of your applicants to accept another position because of poor communications.

If there is any delay, contact the applicant and explain what's happening. People tend to think the worst, if takes longer than you said and they don't hear back from you. The last thing you want is for one of your applicants to accept another position because of poor communications.

Remember, time is of the essence and it's ideal to get the new hire on board as quickly as possible, so they don't find a job elsewhere. If you miss getting the applicant hired, you either have to go with your second (or later) choice or start the process all over again, which costs additional time and resources.

Starting New Employees
It's important that you assign each new employee to an existing team member who is willing and capable of training and mentoring the new team member. This will give them a support system from the very first day. It will provide them with a resource for information and knowledge. It will also help them ease into the position without feeling lost or out of place.

> Assign each new employee to an existing team member who is willing and capable of training and mentoring the new team member.

Starting the first day, you should spend some time with the new employee setting goals and making sure that they understand all the parameters of their job. Begin the process of praising success and reprimanding poor performance as discussed previously.

Chapter 34

Benefiting From Employee Input And Feedback
There are basically two types of feedback that you can receive from employees, and that is simply either positive or negative. How you *determine* which is positive and which is negative, really depends on you and your circumstances.

For example, let's say that you're short-handed and you get feedback (whether solicited or unsolicited) from your employees that they're tired of working short-handed because of vacancies in the team. You could easily consider that to be negative feedback. It may very well be that nobody is more acutely aware of the problem than you. You may be working feverishly to find qualified employees to fill vacant positions. It may be frustrating to have someone else pointing out what is already painfully obvious to you. This type of feedback may even exacerbate the situation, adding to your anxiety and frustration.

However, the employees may see it as providing positive feedback. From their perspective, they may feel as though they are providing you with information they feel is vital to the team / organization, even if it is from their selfish and perhaps narrow perspective of the team dynamics, available resources, your plans, etc.

> How you react to the employee feedback
> will make the difference of whether
> you benefit from the information or not.

How you react to the employee feedback will make the difference of whether you benefit from the information or not. In this particular example, many a manager with this type of feedback would become more frustrated and perhaps even agitated, moody, upset, depressed, etc.

Positively Spinning Feedback
In order to benefit from this type of feedback, it is necessary to put the right *spin* on it. Many people call this "finding the silver lining in a gray cloud" or "making lemonade from lemons." It's a matter of looking at the situation in a way that can be somehow beneficial and then taking action accordingly.

Obviously, in this scenario, being short-handed is never a desirable issue to be dealing with. To a large extent, filling empty positions is somewhat out of your control. You can't magically make qualified employees show up at your place of business. Being short-handed often has a domino effect where other employees get burned out and quit, further exacerbating the problem.

It goes without saying that, you should be doing everything in your power to fill any open positions, but what do you do about the seemingly negative feedback? Rather than heaping it on top of the problem, find the silver lining or make some lemonade. In this case, the silver lining is that the employees are giving you a realistic indication or gauge of their energy level and attitude as it relates to their productivity. From their perspective, by *telling* you how they're being affected, you no longer have to *wonder* how it's affecting them – they "got it off their chest" and now you know.

Once you become aware of any circumstances that are significant, you have the opportunity to make a positive effect on the situation. In this case, you would realize that if you don't have the staff you need, you need to focus immediately on motivating the staff you do have. As I have stated previously, when you take a genuine interest in the success of others, they will reciprocate when the opportunity presents itself.

In this case, it would be a great opportunity to serve up some lemonade by letting the staff know (i.e. be motivational and inspirational) how much you appreciate them and the extra efforts they've put in since becoming short-handed. You could let them know how frustrated you are in being short-handed and that you're making every effort to fill the position(s). Let them know what efforts you are hoping each of them will make to help fill the gaps until new staff members can be hired. During the process of showing appreciation and motivating, ask for a personal commitment, just like when setting goals and performance standards. Simply ask, "can I count on you to <<*extra work needing performed*>> and go the extra mile for me and the team?"

Appreciate The Extra Effort
Always let your people know how much you personally value them and appreciate their extra efforts when they're called to go above and beyond the call of duty. If they respect you and value you as their leader, they will want to help you be successful in your position.

> Let your people know how much you personally value them and appreciate their extra efforts.

If you ever watch sporting events, you've probably seen an injured player return to the game. They're not going back into the game because they enjoy playing hurt, they're doing it for the benefit of others. The coach needs them, the team needs them, the club needs them and the fans need them. Being needed and appreciated is a basic part of the human experience that drives us to try harder and and want to be better.

Inside, athletes aren't any different from you and your people. The only real difference is the "game" that's being played and the field on which it's being executed. In this example, the coach (you) needs them, the team (other employees) needs them, the club (the department, organization, etc.) needs them and the fans (patients, residents and family members) need them. Knowing that they're needed and appreciated can make all the difference in the world to their attitude and willingness to go the extra mile.

Soliciting Employee Input And Feedback

I'm often amazed at how much time is spent by companies and their leaders trying to figure out what other people want or expect from them. There is the external (consumer) side of this, which is facilitated through marketing and advertising. Then there's the internal side of this, which is facilitated through the human resources and employee benefits.

All too often, companies spend much of their efforts on creating plans they believe will benefit their employees and make their company a better place to work than their competitor's. In the process, it often becomes a "father knows best" mentality.

What should be obvious, but for some reason most companies miss this, is that more often than not, the people who are in the best position to provide input on every aspect of the employees are, in fact, the employees themselves. Every issue or concern from employee benefits to working conditions to the tools needed to perform the job can best be revealed through the employees themselves.

Rather than trying to figure out what the employees want or what they don't want, why not just ask them?! That takes the guesswork right out of it. When employees know that they and their contributions are being valued and appreciated, they will readily contribute their perspective and insight.

> Rather than trying to figure out what
> the employees want or what they don't want,
> why not just ask them?!

For example, let's say that there's a sudden decline in production on a particular shift and it isn't readily apparent to you why. Rather than try to determine the problem and fix it by yourself, simply have a brief conversation with all the employees on that shift individually.

Once you've identified the root cause of the problem, more often than not, those same employees will be in a position to provide the fix to the problem. And if not the actual fix, they'll provide the information to get you headed in the right direction. Not surprising, problems frustrate the people affected by them just as much or more than their leaders.

Obviously, there has to be some common sense applied when dealing with problems. If the employees in this example were to tell you that production is suffering because they want to have more pizza parties, that's not the real problem and providing more pizza is not the best solution.

Soliciting employee input and feedback should never be seen as a sign that you don't know what you're doing and you're trying to get the employees to help you do your job. When you approach employees to solicit their feedback, it should come across that;
- You are aware of a situation that is affecting the team (department, organization, etc.).
- You value their insight and perspective regarding the situation.
- You're soliciting their input before you make a final decision as how best to deal with the situation, *because it will affect them*.

> If people know you're looking out for them, they will appreciate and respect you more.

Again, if people know you're looking out for them, they will appreciate and respect you more. NOTE: The "situation" in this case could be an actual problem, potential problem, changes being considered, implementing actual changes, new procedures, etc.

Giving Feedback On The Feedback
Once a decision has been made, relative to employee input and feedback, the results of that decision should be disseminated to the employees. While it's usually best to provide those results in person, it is not always possible to do so. At the very least, a notice or memo should be sent out which details the decision and thanks the employees for their input and reiterates the value you place on their input and feedback.

Having an open, two-way flow of input and feedback from the employees to their superiors not only encourages a higher level of conscious and critical thinking in the workplace, but it also stimulates improved performance, self-leadership and overall satisfaction with their job and the workplace in general. It promotes an over-all healthier business environment that is beneficial to everyone.

Input And Feedback On A Personal Level
The same approach of employee input and feedback can be taken on a more personal level as well. Taking an opportunity to gain further insight into your people's lives need not be limited to problems or changes happening in the workplace.

For example, if you notice that Jane doesn't seem to be her usual positive and jovial self, you might inquire as to why. You could simply say something like, "Hey Jane, I noticed that you don't seem to be yourself today, is something bothering you?"

Whether something is bothering Jane or not, she now knows that you're aware of her on a more personal level. She knows that you've taken a personal interest in her well being. Whether you can help out or not, Jane knows that you're observant of and concerned about her as a person.

Simply acknowledging a subtle difference in someone, whether it's attitude, appearance, behavior, etc. can make a big difference in a person's life. It may not be a matter of solving a problem or making any significant difference in their lives. But taking a personal interest in people can make a big difference in their attitude, appreciation, and respect for you, which money simply cannot buy.

> Taking a personal interest in people can make a big difference in their attitude, appreciation, and respect for you, which money simply cannot buy.

This is especially true if you notice something or comment about something that would be seen as a positive attribute or a genuine and sincere compliment. Something as simple as inquiring about a person's family (i.e. children, grand children, etc.) can really make their day. Going out of your way to do something or say something expressive of appreciation or genuine concern will go a long way.

Using Suggestion Boxes Effectively
Many companies use suggestion boxes or comment boxes to solicit feedback from their customers regarding their experiences. In today's technological world, telephone or online questionnaires and surveys have replaced the physical boxes in many organizations.

Many other companies elect not to have any type of formal input and feedback system for their employees to convey their thoughts, suggestions, ideas, or in many instances, complaints. For many organizations, a suggestion box could be more accurately renamed as a "complaint box."

Any organization where the suggestion box would contain mostly complaints could most likely be characterized as the antithesis of what this book represents. The purpose of this book is to create an environment where everyone is working together for the common good of all, CEO and front line employees alike.

When everyone is working together for the common good, what benefits one, benefits all. At the same time, what hurts one, hurts all, either directly or indirectly. Therefore, it is essential that the executives and leaders truly understand their employees and their perspective, both good and bad.

> When everyone is working together for the common good, what benefits one, benefits all.

Simply ignoring the bad does not make it go away. In fact, ignoring problems usually leads to greater problems that are more catastrophic in nature. It's like the joke where some people are sitting around talking about their cars. One person is complaining that they heard a knocking sound coming from the engine, took it to a repair shop and now the car needs repaired. Another person chimes in and says they used to have that same problem, but no longer. The first person asks what they did to fix the problem, to which the second person says, "I just turned up the radio!"

Masking a problem, ignoring it, or drowning it out won't make it go away. Sure, you may not hear it or think about it any longer, but it's still there and left unaddressed, it will get much worse. When considering a solution, throwing a "one size fits all" fix at it may not help at all. Addressing the problem and resolving it in a satisfactory manner is the only way to hope that it will be fixed.

> Masking a problem, ignoring it, or drowning it out won't make it go away.

Admitting Problems Is Not Failure

Admitting that your team, department or organization has problems is not admitting that you're a failure. It's simply acknowledging the fact that there are issues regarding your operation that need to be addressed and resolved. The resolution may involve efforts on your (and the organization's) part, the employees' part or a combination of both, resulting in some sort of compromise.

Complaints in general, whether they be from your customers or your employees should be seen as an opportunity to make your organization better. If it is indeed a legitimate complaint, you have the opportunity to fix it. You can solicit input and feedback from the person(s) who are in the best position to help you resolve the problem.

If, on the other hand, the complaint is not legitimate and/or incendiary in nature, malicious, discriminatory, etc., then you still have an opportunity to make the organization better. In this case, the fix would probably involve determining the disgruntled employee(s) and dealing effectively with them. The solution to such a problem may very well include the separation of employment, if that's ultimately what is required.

Regardless of the nature of input and feedback that you may receive from employees directly or via a suggestion box (or other venue), it is important that you don't ignore them.

> Employees want and need to know that there is an avenue available to them to sound off.

Employees want and need to know that there is an avenue available to them to sound off. They want and need to know that someone will listen to (or read) their input and feedback. They want and need to know that their voices are being heard. They want and need to know that someone cares.

Obviously, you can't go around and tell everyone how you considered each and every comment that was placed in the suggestion box. However, you can summarize the employee input on a regular basis in the form of a note, memo, or periodic in-service or training meeting. Don't minimize any legitimate input and always show your appreciation for the employees and their legitimate suggestions.

Conducting Effective Exit Interviews
Another way of gathering information from employees is through effective exit interviews. Try to have a standardized form or set of questions that you ask of all exiting employees. That way you can analyze the trends to see if there is any consistency in the underlying cause of your people leaving.

Many organizations don't like to conduct exit interviews, because they believe the departing employees are not being entirely objective. Others simply don't want to know what's on the mind of the employee who is "abandoning ship," because they take it as a personal assault. Still others see it as direct criticism to their own management and leadership abilities, or the lack thereof.

Look For Ways To Improve
As with everything else we've discussed, about employee input and feedback, even negative comments can be used to make positive changes.

> Take criticism as an opportunity to re-evaluate yourself and your leadership techniques.

Any time an employee <u>voluntarily</u> leaves your organization, you should do an exit interview. Regardless of what a departing employee has to say, whether good or bad, whether disgruntled or not, whether objective or not, it's important to know what and how they are feeling about leaving and what factors led them to that decision.

Even if the employee sharply criticizes you or your methods of management and leadership, it's important to listen. Criticism is always hard to take, especially if you are a person who is dedicated to helping others succeed. Remember, not all criticism is valid and some of it may be way off base.

Take criticism as an opportunity to re-evaluate yourself and your leadership techniques. If you find that the criticism is valid, eliminate the undesirable issue and take steps to work a more positive habit into your skill set.

You should know going into an exit interview that there exists a significant possibility that not everything the departing employee will say is true, much less accurate or realistic. However, there is a distinct probability that some of what is said can be used to bring about positive changes. After the interview, you can "glean the wheat from the chaff" to see if there is any legitimacy to any negative comments made.

It's worth noting here that anger is typically a secondary emotion in most people. When someone is angry, there is usually an underlying primary emotion manifested as anger. For example, an employee may have a fear of not being accepted and respected by the team, who acts out angrily or aggressively towards other team members.

> When someone is angry, there is usually an underlying primary emotion manifested as anger.

When conducting exit interviews with angry people, you may want to probe deeper to expose the primary cause of their anger. Quite often, it's fear that is the underlying cause. Again, the root cause of any problem is essential to eliminating the problem and not simply treating the symptoms.

Don't Ask Unless You're Prepared To Address It
Perhaps the most important thing to consider when dealing with employee input and feedback is that of taking action. Not soliciting employee input and feedback is a mistake. Ignoring legitimate concerns or not acknowledging them is an even bigger mistake. Acknowledging them, but then doing nothing about it is by far the biggest mistake of all.

The reality is that if you want to make your organization better, you have to see employee input and feedback as a resource, just like any other resource. Ignoring it or failing to address it is a huge mistake. On the other hand, effectively dealing with this resource will have a positive effect on your organization.

Effective leaders know that open communications are essential for the accomplishment of goals and improved attitude and performance. Effectively dealing with problems from any source ultimately leads to an environment that is more conducive for success. The greater the opportunity for success, the more likely it will happen and the easier it will be to accomplish.

> Effectively dealing with problems from any source ultimately leads to an environment that is more conducive for success.

Chapter 35

Lady Justice Is Blind, You Shouldn't Be
Managers (and to some extent, all employees) are agents of the company or organization for whom they are employed. As such, they have certain legal, ethical and moral duties and responsibilities. People in healthcare are held to a higher standard in the discharge and performance of their responsibilities and duties. Therefore, you should always perform your job duties with your eyes wide open concerning these matters.

Don't Let Your Guard Down
Because of the litigious nature of our society, you cannot afford to let your guard down or approach your responsibilities with any degree of casualness or lack of preparation. In fact, you should imagine that you will be sued.

Imagine yourself as the defendant in a legal case, maybe something as horrible as a wrongful death law suit. Imagine what it would be like to lose any professional licenses that you possess and the effect that would have on your livelihood. Unless your actions, words and deeds are above reproach at all times, that's the risk that you allow to be omnipresent.

In heath care, practically every aspect of the industry has to do with another person's health and well being. Each and every action you make or inaction on your part, is subject to scrutiny and review. Every word or absence of proper wording or documentation can potentially expose one to liabilities and risk of litigation.

> Each and every action you make or inaction on your part, is subject to scrutiny and review.

Being a manager, leader or simply having some supervisory responsibilities over company resources (including human resources) puts you in a potentially litigious situation. Potentially, everything that is done or not done by others under your supervision or control subjects you to legal scrutiny and review.

Therefore, as a strategic element of management and leadership, this knowledge should not only be kept constantly in your mind, but used as a behavioral modifier in your daily activities. This applies not only to actions and interactions with others, but all behavior and communications as well.

This applies not only to people in a management or supervisory position, but to every person in the organization where a liability issue may be present or could arise. Every employee should be aware of the importance of their conduct and communication in relation to potential legal issues and liabilities.

Leading A Horse To Water
It's been said that, "you can lead a horse to water, but you can't make it drink." The same can be said of people, in that, "you can lead a person to the waters of opportunity and success, but you can't make them drink."

It is important to remember that as a leader, it is **not** your job to make everyone around you successful. It may very well be your *desire*, but it isn't your job or your responsibility. You personally can't do that and you really shouldn't be fixated on that specific aspect of your business plan, goals and personal growth.

> As a leader, it is **not** your job to
> make everyone around you successful.

Your job as an effective leader is simply to provide the direction, tools, resources and opportunity (the water) for others to be successful (to drink). Whether or not they choose to drink and how deeply they choose to drink from those waters of success is entirely up to them.

Alexander Pope had this concept in mind when he penned his famous poem about learning, knowledge and understanding;
> A little learning is a dang'rous thing;
> Drink deep, or taste not the Pierian spring:
> There shallow draughts intoxicate the brain,
> And drinking largely sobers us again.

In Greek mythology, the Pierian Spring was the source of great knowledge and inspiration, and by drinking its waters, it was believed that one would gain great wisdom and understanding. Pope is also instructing us that drinking (i.e. learning, engaging, etc.) a small amount can "intoxicate" a person so that they feel as though they know a lot more than they really do.

However, when drinking largely (i.e. gaining great knowledge, engaging with full purpose and determination, etc.) it "sobers" a person in the real perspective that they have a greater understanding (and knowledge, experience, etc.) so that they become "grounded."

When a person gains a real perspective of their own knowledge, understanding, experience, etc., they realize that they haven't yet, and possibly never will reach the pinnacle of greatness, because it is virtually a never-ending quest.

Gaining Greater Knowledge And Understanding
Being an effective leader means that you must drink deeply from the Pierian Spring and encourage the same from those around you. The more you and the people that surround you learn, understand, know and are capable of, the better off the entire group will be, which ultimately benefits everyone, including the organization and ultimately the patients, residents and families.

Chapter 36

Put And Keep The Odds In Your Favor
You've probably heard it said that, "life is a gamble." That's true, in large part, because we can't control every aspect of our lives. In fact, there are times when we have little control over what happens in our lives, much less the lives of others. However, as with cards, dice or life, the better you can stack the odds in your favor, the greater the chances are of a favorable outcome.

Don't Rely On Luck
There may be elements of life that could be considered luck. For example, a good employee who's looking for a job at the same time you're advertising a job opening. But don't depend on luck, even though it may occasionally favor you. You may have heard it said that, "luck has a peculiar habit of favoring those who don't depend on it."

> Luck has a peculiar habit of favoring those who don't depend on it.

Even though you can't guarantee the exact outcome of the success you desire for yourself and others, there are things you can and should do to put and keep the odds of success in your favor. Don't leave it up to chance- be proactive.

Chart your path (and those of your employees) with achievable goals as mile stones. And above all, use this book as a road map for realizing those goals and the success you desire on your journey.

Divide And Conquer Your Dreams
"Success" may be the word that you use to encompass the goals and achievements you envision, but in and of itself it can't be

accomplished without first *dividing and conquering* each aspect and element of the vision you have of your success.

Whatever the improvements you want for yourself or others, you first have to determine what is desired versus what is actually being done, and then creating a working plan to bridge that gap. For example, if you want better teamwork, you have to specifically quantify where you want the teamwork behaviors to be. Then identify where the behaviors are now.

Next, make a workable plan to bridge that gap and bring the existing behavior up to the expected behavior. It doesn't matter if it's employee performance, customer service, teamwork, or anything else, the principles are still the same.

The greatest common denominator in almost every aspect of the business that any organization conducts is people. The one thing that is true of almost every organization is that the people do make the difference. Whether it's good or bad, it all comes back to people. Whether it's the employees or the leaders, somewhere along the line, people are making the difference.

As a leader, the only way to succeed is by and through successful people. Machines and technology may make things easier, but it ultimately comes down to people.

> As a leader, the only way to succeed is by and through successful people.

Employee Satisfaction
Perhaps one of the most critical factors in creating an environment that provides real and substantive opportunities for success is that of employee satisfaction. Employee satisfaction can be summed up as how employees generally feel about the work they're

performing and the amount gratification, pleasure or contentment they derive from that work.

The employees of today are much different from the employees of the past. A couple of generations ago, people often spent their entire working lives at a single company. There was an obligation that was felt on their part to be loyal and committed to the company. That was the standard in society and it's what was expected from your average, honest, hard working "regular folks."

A generation ago, the employee mentality was that hard work and long hours would get you where you wanted to go. There wasn't so much company loyalty in employees, and changing jobs was common place, often the means to the end. The "end" in this case being a more desirable position, higher income, better social stature, etc.

Greatness Or Just Average
There will always be those who aspire to greatness in any generation, but the average employees of today are interested in something much different from those of the past. Employees today are interested in having a simpler, less complicated life. They care more about having time off to do the things they enjoy, rather than spending their lives scraping and clawing their way to the top of the heap. They care more about their social contacts than their social stature. For the current generation of employees, "less is more." They want less stress and more satisfaction.

> Employees today are interested in having a simpler, less complicated life.

It's been said that, "even if you win the rat race, you're still a rat." The employees of today aren't interested in being rats. They're more interested in being "fat cats." That's not to say that they're lazy, but rather that they prefer a balanced and perhaps more leisurely life where it's not "all work and no play." Where work is not the focus of life, but rather the trade-off or the means to an end, where the "end" is their idyllic life.

A major news article revealed that employees value coworkers and personal control over compensation. It said that, "...the three components of a job that employees overwhelmingly responded were the most important factors in keeping them happy were:
- The specific tasks a job entails on a day-to-day basis.
- How much control the employee has over his or her daily tasks.
- Relationships with co-workers and customers, including supervisors and colleagues."

The article went on to say that, "...the research shows that money is not enough to keep good employees happy. From the employer's perspective, realizing salary is not one of the key drivers of workplace happiness can help employers focus on the areas which will drive job satisfaction to create a happier environment for all."
- *Forbes.com*

> Research shows that money is not enough to keep good employees happy.

You will notice that the factors employees consider to be most important in their satisfaction are those that can be achieved through the successful implementation of the proven concepts and strategies contained in this book.

CONCLUSION

It may not be immediately obvious how each of the techniques contained in this book (such as effective interviewing and hiring, etc.) will help develop self-leadership in others. However, each aspect of the human relations interaction should work together, either directly or indirectly to create an environment and a system of positive results in the workplace that will assist you in leading others to self-leadership.

Think of it this way- it's a lot easier to get where you're going if your vehicle is tuned up, has good windshield wipers, lights, no flat tires, etc. The same is true for other travelers on the same road.

Being an effective leader is not a difficult thing. While it may take some extra effort in the beginning, the results are worth every bit of effort it takes;
- You will be able to accomplish more in a day than ever before.
- You will spend less time putting out fires and more time with your other responsibilities.
- Your employees will waste less time and spend more time working on their own success.

As a result of successful implementation;
- Morale and job satisfaction will increase.
- Turn over and absenteeism will decrease.
- Quantity and productivity will improve.
- Quality and performance will improve.
- Customer Service will improve.

> While it may take some extra effort in the beginning, the results are worth every bit of effort it takes.

WHAT'S NEXT?

It doesn't matter if you're the CEO or front line employee, the best thing you can do is to make a difference. Confucius provided some excellent advice when he said, "The essence of knowledge is, having it, to use it." It doesn't matter what your position, the information in this book will help the entire organization. Share this knowledge with others and implement it into your organization.

You've probably heard it said that, "if it's going to be, it's up to me." Even if others in your organization don't catch the vision right away, let it work for you and you be the example. When successfully implemented, the results will be positive and productive.

As you begin to experience the benefits that can be derived from this book, share your experiences and recommend it to others.

> If it's going to be, it's up to me.

As you consider the use of these techniques, think of this book as a recipe- much like a recipe for a cake. It takes each of the different ingredients (i.e. individual techniques) combined together to achieve the final product. Omission of one or more of the ingredients may result in an undesirable product or one that leaves a bad taste in your mouth.

However, if you correctly mix all the necessary ingredients, you will have a great cake. Once you have a great cake recipe, you can add other "extras" such as chocolate (or other) flavorings, fruits, pudding or ice cream in the center and various icings on the cake!

With that in mind, good luck and bon appetite!

Appendix A

Part I

Critical Factors / Interviewing Questions

As you go through the interview process, realize that experience does not necessarily take precedence over potential. However, previous experience may demonstrate a persons capacity to perform their duties, whereas the inexperienced person is presently unproven in the ability to perform the job. Even though skills and job duties can be taught, a person's personality, attitude and core values cannot.

The following is a basic list of critical factors that should be considered during an interview, particularly the front-line employees. They can be weighted according to the importance or desirability of a particular quality or qualification. For example, Honesty and Integrity may be an extremely critical factor to you and you may give it a weight of 2 while you may assign Qualifications a weight of 1 because it isn't as important to you.

Below each critical factor is a basic list of questions that may be considered during an interview. While this is by no means a definitive list, it does provide a basis from which you can expand to cover the various needs of your particular situation and hiring needs.

Pick some of these questions (it's not necessary to ask all of them) and modify as needed to create your own specific list(s) for conducting interviews. It may be beneficial to have separate critical factor / interviewing sheets for each position.

Additionally, you should consider some "situational" interview questions to ask applicants. These types of questions demonstrate the applicant's ability (or perhaps lack thereof) to quickly assess problems and "think on their feet." Situational questions can include hypothetical scenarios or actual events that have happened in your organization in the past. Examples might include the following;

> (1) You've just arrived at work and <<*describe scenario / problem*>> What would you do? Explain.
>
> (2) At the end of your shift <<*describe scenario / problem #1*>> and <<*describe scenario / problem #2*>> happen simultaneously. How do you prioritize which problem to address first and how do you ensure that both problems are brought to a satisfactory conclusion?
>
> (3) Your supervisor comes to you and <<*describe scenario / problem*>> What would you do? Explain.
>
> (4) A customer complains to you that <<*describe scenario / problem*>> What would you do? Explain.
>
> (5) A coworker <<*describe scenario / problem*>> What would you do? Explain.
>
> (6) You Witness another employee <<*describe scenario / problem*>> What would you do? Explain.

In some of the interview questions you will see two or more **bold** words separated by a slash (e.g. "What things tend to make your attitude **better** / **worse** regarding work?"). Questions written this way are meant to provide multiple questions in one, where each **bold** word could be used singularly in the question.

In this example, you have the two separate questions; "What things tend to make your attitude *__better__* regarding work?" and "What things tend to make your attitude *__worse__* regarding work?"

Critical Factors / Basic Questions For All Positions

Part A of this appendix addresses the basic critical factors and interviewing questions, while Part B addresses additional critical factors and interviewing questions for key (i.e. beyond front-line employee) positions.

There are basic factors that are critical to consider when interviewing applicants for any position within your organization. Just because one position may not be as essential or important as another position within the organization, doesn't mean that it doesn't deserve the same significance when considering applicants. If you treat each position as if it were the most important position, you will raise the quality standards of all employees, not just those in key positions.

These sample questions are not meant to be yes/no questions, even though some appear to be. If a yes/no answer is given, ask the applicant to further explain their answer by simply saying, "explain that further for me" or "give me some more details" or "how did that turn out," etc. Encourage details and explanation when necessary in order to get accurate information.

A "Critical Factor Review Sheet" example is included at the end of this appendix for your convenience.

NOTE: This list is arranged in alphabetical order for convenience purposes only;

Ambition

Considerations
Is this person ambitious and do they exhibit enthusiasm along with persistence? Is their ambition focused, targeted and balanced with common sense and a clear head? Do they appear to have a genuine interest in working with your organization or are they just there to put in some time and get a paycheck?

Interview Questions
- ► How do you define "ambition?"
- ► How ambitious are you?
- ► How would your **mother / father / previous boss** describe your ambition towards work?
- ► What have you accomplished of significance over the past year?

Appearance

Considerations
Where appearance and personal presentation are important, does this person present themselves well? Are they properly groomed and clothed? Do they project the image that your organization is striving for? Or are they sloppy or unconcerned with their appearance and presence?

Interview Questions
- ► <<*Ask questions that would be appropriate, if necessary*>>

Attitude

Considerations
Does this person demonstrate a positive, caring attitude? Does this person have a willingness to put forth the effort and commitment to fit in with your organization? Can you visualize this person positively affecting your organization and your vision? Or does this person seem to have an entitlement attitude where they're interested more in what's in it for them than what they can bring to the table to you and the organization?

Interview Questions
- ► How do you define "good attitude?"
- ► How would your **mother / father / previous boss** describe your attitude towards work?
- ► What things tend to make your attitude **better / worse** regarding work?

Behavior

Considerations
Is this person's behavior consistent with the way they're selling you on themselves? Is their behavior calm or disruptive? Is their behavior amiable or confrontational? Is their behavior consistent with your goals and vision? Or are they simply telling you what they think you want to hear?

Interview Questions
- ▶ What would you consider to be inappropriate behavior at work?
- ▶ Have you ever behaved inappropriately at work?
- ▶ Have you ever witnessed inappropriate behavior at work, and if so, what happened?
- ▶ Would your **mother / father / previous boss** describe your behavior as **calm or disruptive / amiable or confrontational**?

Cooperation

Considerations
Is this person willing to cooperate with others in order to accomplish their work? Are they personable and likable? Can they work well with others and be respectful of those around them? Are they helpful and willing to help others on the team? Do they maintain self-control, even in difficult situations or when asked to go above and beyond the call of duty? Or are they self-centered, disrespectful or see themselves in a dominant or individual (i.e. "maverick" or "lone wolf") role?

Interview Questions
- ▶ How do you define "cooperation?"
- ▶ Tell me of a difficult work-related experience where your cooperation was instrumental in success – what did you learn from this experience?
- ▶ Tell me of a difficult work-related experience where the lack of cooperation of another person seriously hampered the situation and what did you learn from this experience?
- ▶ Tell me of a time where a co-worker made a bad decision or

mistake and you had to help fix things – how did it turn out?
▶ Do you work better by yourself or with others as a team?

Customer Service

Considerations

Does this person know that customers are the reason for our work and not a distraction to it? Can they provide exceptional customer service to both external and internal customers? Do they look for ways to improve customer service? Are they willing to put in extra effort to provide excellent customer service? Can they balance customer service with organizational policies and procedures? Are they enthusiastic about gaining more customers? Or do they believe that simply doing a good job is where their commitment to customer service ends?

Interview Questions
▶ How do you define "good customer service?"
▶ What's the most important aspect of good customer service?
▶ Which is more important, good customer service or company standards and policy?
▶ Tell me of a time when you went above and beyond the call of duty to provide good customer service.
▶ Tell me of a time when a customer was very angry and how you reacted - what was the outcome?
▶ What can you personally do to improve customer service and bring more clients or customers in?

Dependability

Considerations

Can this person be depended upon to show up for work on time, each and every shift and be ready to work? Can they be depended upon to do the work they are responsible for? Are they willing to help out when and where they are needed? Or do they take a casual approach to their job and see it as interfering with their lives?

Interview Questions
- ▶ How do you define "dependability?"
- ▶ Why is dependability important?
- ▶ How would you convince me that you are a dependable person?
- ▶ How would your previous boss describe your dependability?
- ▶ Our needs are <<*describe anticipated work hours and work schedule*>>, do you see any conflicts with this kind of work schedule?
- ▶ Occasionally, we need our employees to work overtime, would that be a problem for you?

Education
Considerations
If there is an educational requirement, does this person have verifiable evidence of all educational certifications claimed? Does this person exhibit a knowledge commensurate with the level of education claimed? In addition to "book smarts" does this person have common sense and creativity? Or is this person simply decorating their resume or application with misrepresentations or outright lies?

Interview Questions
- ▶ What are your feelings about people who are continually learning and improving themselves?
- ▶ Do you think education is an important aspect of job performance?
- ▶ Which do you think is more important, education or experience?
- ▶ What can you tell me about <<*something of importance that is essential to the job*>>?

Experience
Considerations
Where applicable, does this person have the necessary experience? Is the experience quantifiable and/or verifiable? Can they clearly demonstrate and explain with an intimate and first-hand knowledge

of all experience they claim? Or are they operating under the concept of, "if you can't dazzle them with brilliance then baffle them with bull!"

Interview Questions
- ▶ What experience do you have that would be beneficial to our organization?
- ▶ Which do you think is more important, education or experience?
- ▶ What has your experience been with <<*something of importance that is essential to the job*>>?
- ▶ What is the most important aspect of your experience and skills?
- ▶ Tell me of a time when you had to learn something new on the job.
- ▶ Tell me of a time when you helped a co-worker learn something new on the job.

Expertise

Considerations
Does this person have any quantifiable and verifiable expertise that would be beneficial to you and/or the organization? Are they proficient in their areas of knowledge and/or skills enough to competently teach others? If so, how would it be beneficial to you and the organization?

Interview Questions
- ▶ Are you an expert in anything related to our organization?
- ▶ What makes you an expert?
- ▶ Do others believe that you're an expert?
- ▶ How has that expertise benefited you in the past?
- ▶ Tell me of a time when you trained a co-worker or improved a co-worker's knowledge or skills.
- ▶ How will you use your expertise to benefit our organization?

Fear

Considerations

Does this person exhibit any fear, reluctance, apprehension or concerns in regards any aspect of the job for which they are being considered? Are they withdrawn or introverted? Or are they outgoing, extroverted, confident and ready to jump in with vigor?

Interview Questions

- What frightens you the most about <<*job being applied for, duties of job, demands, etc.*>>?
- Does anything frighten you about working with our **organization / employees / customers**?
- Do you have any concerns about the **job requirements / our goals / fitting in with team or organization**?

Goals

Considerations

Does this person have any career goals? Are they ambitious and do they focus on reaching those goals? Do their goals resonate with your goals and the organizations goals? Have they set and reached goals in the past? If so, how did they reach those goals and what was the outcome? Or are they just trying to get by with the least amount of effort and take each day as it comes, without a plan?

Interview Questions

- How do you define "goals?"
- Are goals important to you?
- What goals have you set for yourself **short-term (i.e. 0-6 months) / long-term (6months – 5+ years)**?
- What significant goals have you accomplished in the past – how did you reach them?
- Of all the things you could be in life, why did you choose this career path?

Honesty & Integrity

Considerations

Can this person be trusted to work in your facility, around your equipment and supplies, with your existing staff and around your customers? Are they honest and trustworthy? Do they maintain eye contact when speaking? Or does this person seem to be hiding something or misrepresenting anything important in any way?

Interview Questions
- ▶ How do you define "integrity?"
- ▶ Is integrity important in the workplace? Explain.
- ▶ Would you consider taking a pen from work as being dishonest?
- ▶ Would you consider taking extra minutes on break or lunch as being dishonest?
- ▶ How would your previous boss describe your integrity?
- ▶ Tell me of a time when your integrity benefited you or the organization.
- ▶ Tell me of a time when a co-worker's lack of integrity caused a problem for the organization.

Initiative

Considerations

Is this person a self-starter? Does this person see things that need to be done and then take the initiative to accomplish the work? Does this person look for things to do or ask for things to do? Or do they only put forth the minimum effort and work that is required and wait to be told to do anything extra or out of their routine?

Interview Questions
- ▶ How do you define "initiative?"
- ▶ What gets you going at the start of your day?
- ▶ How would your **mother / father / previous boss** describe your initiative?
- ▶ What do you do if you have free time at work?

Job Knowledge

Considerations
Does this person possess a sufficient knowledge and understanding needed to perform the job. Do they have any formal or certified training or experience that is verifiable? Does their knowledge demonstrate any proficiency in the job? Would they be able to train another person who has no such knowledge? Or is their knowledge insufficient or incomplete?

Interview Questions
- *<<Ask questions that test the knowledge of the applicant, regarding various aspects of the job>>*

Manageability

Considerations
Is this person manageable? Will they take direction willingly or will they try to manage you? Will they respect you and your position of authority? Or will they be resistant to directives or constantly be trying to go around you and straight to your boss or others of authority?

Interview Questions
- Are you a leader, follower or independent? Explain.
- Is the organizational hierarchy important to performing your job duties?
- Does your last boss know more or less than you about your job?
- Is it important for you to have organizational policies and procedures or does that interfere with your ability to work more efficiently?

Performance

Considerations
Can this person consistently perform the expected job duties at the expected performance level? Can they work well independently without constant supervision? Can they perform well under pressure? Or is their performance inconsistent and varied

according to external variables?

Interview Questions
- ▶ Do you work better in an environment that is more structured or less structured?
- ▶ Do you tend to work more independently or try to stay in stride with the rest of the group?
- ▶ How does being under pressure affect your work?
- ▶ What one factor would produce better performance in your work?

Personality

Considerations
Is this person a team player? Are they personable? Are they amiable? Are they respectful? Will they fit in well with your team? Or are there potential problems that can be seen even before they start?

Interview Questions
- ▶ Would you consider yourself to be outgoing?
- ▶ How would your friends describe your personality?
- ▶ How do you handle new situations or environments?
- ▶ What is the single most important aspect of your personality that makes you who you are?
- ▶ If you could be any zoo animal, what would you be and why?
NOTE: The answer to this question is supposed to be (according to psychology) an indication of how the person answering the question perceives how others see them.

Qualifications

Considerations
Does this person have at least the minimal experience, education, aptitude, training, understanding, knowledge and skills to fill the position? Do they have a probable and realistic potential to learn and achieve the necessary minimal performance standards? Is there a likelihood that they can consistently perform above the

minimal performance standards?

Interview Questions
- ▶ Why do you think you are qualified for this job?
- ▶ Why should I pick you over all the other applicants?
- ▶ If there is one thing you could change about your qualifications, what would it be and how would that be beneficial?
- ▶ Do you think you are **under / over** qualified for this job?
- ▶ If you were to start working productive today, what is the **first / last** thing you would do?

Reliability

Considerations
Will this person give the appropriate significance and value to their professional career and make their job a priority in their life? Can this person be counted on to be where they're supposed to be, when they're supposed to be there? Can they be counted on to do what they're supposed to do when they're supposed to do it. Can they be counted on to do their job as it's supposed to be done? Or are they hit and miss or hot and cold?

Interview Questions
- ▶ How do you rank your job and career in relation to other priorities in your life?
- ▶ Are you reliable? If so, give me some examples to demonstrate your reliability.
- ▶ How many days do you feel is an acceptable number to miss from work?
- ▶ How many days from work have you missed in the past year?
- ▶ Have you worked with anyone who was absent a lot? If so, how did it affect **you / the team / department / organization**?
- ▶ How important is punctuality to you?
- ▶ Are you ever late to work? If so, what causes you to be late?

Responsibility

Considerations

Does this person exhibit any signs of loyalty and dedication? Do they have good time management skills and complete work timely? Are they responsible and take ownership of their behavior and performance? Or are they quick to pass the buck and blame their circumstances or others for their short comings?

Interview Questions

- ▶ Do you feel that you are a dedicated and loyal employee? If so, give me some examples to demonstrate your dedication and loyalty.
- ▶ What do you do when you make a mistake?
- ▶ How do you take personal responsibility for your work?
- ▶ Tell me of a time when you made a mistake and what you did to resolve it.

Risk Taking

Considerations

Does this person avoid taking any unnecessary risks? Is their risk level conservative or liberal? Do they demonstrate maturity in their approach to work? Are they looking out for the best interests of others or the organization? Do they learn from the experiences of others? Do they "look before they leap?" Or do they approach their work carelessly or with reckless abandon?

Interview Questions

- ▶ Are you a risk taker at work? If so, give me some examples of risks you have taken and their outcome.
- ▶ Has there ever been a time at work where you had to take a risk in order to get your job done? If yes, explain.
- ▶ What is the single greatest lesson you have learned from your own mistakes?
- ▶ What is the single greatest lesson you have learned from the mistakes of others?

Safety

Considerations

Does this person follow all safety policies and procedures? Can they effectively assess potential safety issues? Do they utilize all necessary safety equipment and supplies at all times? Do they avoid any activity that might put themselves or others at personal risk? Or are they sloppy and haphazard in their activities, throwing caution to the wind?

Interview Questions
- ▶ Explain to me your understanding of safety in the workplace and why it's important for everyone.
- ▶ Do you abide by all safety standards and guidelines while at work?
- ▶ Do you use all safety equipment and follow all safety procedures?
- ▶ Tell me of a time when you witnessed another person who ignored established safety procedures that had negative consequences. What should have been done differently?
- ▶ What is the most important thing you can do to ensure the safety of yourself and others around you?

Scheduling

Considerations

Does this person have other commitments that conflict with scheduled work hours? Is this person punctual and take their job seriously? Can this person be expected to reliably fill the position on the required shift without creating additional scheduling problems? Or are there possible conflicts that would negatively affect the organization?

Interview Questions
- ▶ The scheduling for the open position is <<*describe schedule requirements, any overtime or holiday requirements, etc.*>>. Can you work this schedule without conflicts that would cause you to be late or miss work?

- ▶ Do you foresee any possible conflicts with the schedule (shifts, hours, overtime, holidays, etc.)?
- ▶ How do you handle conflicts with work and other demands on your time?
- ▶ Are you flexible in your time to work other shifts if needed?

Sense of Urgency

Considerations
Does this person have the mental and physical capacity to work in a demanding environment, with attention to detail, as needed to achieve performance standards? Can they remain focused? Are they alert and attentive to the various aspects of the job? Or are they easily distracted or seem disinterested, aloof or preoccupied?

Interview Questions
- ▶ What does it mean to you to have a "sense of urgency?"
- ▶ How do you prioritize job duties, assignments, tasks along with unexpected issues that must be included in your work?
- ▶ How do you decide what needs immediate attention and what can be put off until later?
- ▶ Tell me of a time when something came up that was urgent and you took care of the matter before it became a problem.
- ▶ Tell me of a time when something came up where another person did not take care of an urgent matter and it became a bigger problem, what was it, what was done, what was the outcome?

Appendix A

Part II

Critical Factors For Key Positions

When you are interviewing for key positions (i.e. executive, managerial, administrative or other positions of added responsibility, trust, etc.), your list should include additional items of concern that will help you evaluate the applicant's value, based upon their actual experience, knowledge and skill set. Again, they can be weighted according to the importance or desirability of a particular quality or qualification. As with the Part A of this appendix, you should include "situational" interview questions.

A "Critical Factor Review Sheet" example is included at the end of this appendix for your convenience.

NOTE: This list is arranged in alphabetical order for convenience purposes only;

Approachability

Considerations
Is this person easily approachable by employees, peers, superiors and customers alike in a non-threatening and non-demeaning way? Is their demeanor one of genuine caring and concern? Do they appreciate input and feedback? Or do they seem disinterested or feel their time is more important and valuable than those around them?

Interview Questions
▶ In your dealings with people, would you say others have difficulty or no difficulty in approaching you? To what do you attribute the difficult or not difficult aspect of your approachability?

- Do you believe there is no such thing as a stupid question? Explain.
- What do you see as the pros and cons of having an "open door" policy?
- How do you feel about "suggestion boxes?"
- Do you think customer surveys or comment cards provide any benefit? Explain.

Assertiveness

Considerations

Is this person confident and not easily intimidated by others, including those of authority? Do they have the necessary assertiveness to assume a dominant presence in the workplace as a leader without being overbearing or becoming angry? Can this person confront issues and problems directly and thoroughly to resolution? Or does this person take a casual or even avoidance attitude to their authoritative role or do they become become angry and/or overbearing?

Interview Questions

- Would you consider yourself more of a leader or follower? If leader, give some examples.
- Has there ever been a situation where someone has confronted you and intimidated you? If yes, explain.
- How do you deal with confrontation?
- How do you get others to do what you want them to do?
- Would you describe your leadership style as being more democratic or autocratic? Explain.
- How would others describe your leadership style – democratic or autocratic? Explain.
- Are you easily angered? If yes, what does it take to get you angry and what is eventual outcome?

Communication

Considerations

Does this person communicate effectively, both downward and

upward as well? Are they direct, clear and understandable? Do they understand the importance of clarity in their communications? Are they effective in their written communication, able to make points and summarize in a concise manner? Can they explain complex information so that it is easily understood? Or do they leave others confused or unsure of what they're trying to convey?

Interview Questions
- How do you communicate with **subordinates / peers / superiors** in **verbal / written** communications?
- Tell me of a time when you had to explain something technical to someone who did not understand the technical jargon.
- Tell me of a time when you had to communicate something sensitive to your boss, how you handled it and what was the outcome?
- Tell me of a time when you had to communicate detailed and complex information to others in a way that was easily understandable and executable.
- Tell me of a time when some communication (from you or another person) was misunderstood and created a problem. What was the consequence and how was the problem resolved?

Confidence

Considerations
Does this person have the self confidence necessary to successfully lead others and help others to improve themselves, and do it in a calm manner? Does this person trust in their own abilities and reasonably expect the results they desire? Does this person have confidence in their personal knowledge and skill set? Or will they need constant assurance in order to be effective? Does this person tend to be even the slightest uncertain or introverted?

Interview Questions
- What are your greatest **strengths / weaknesses** and how will they affect your performance in this job?
- Give me some examples that would demonstrate your

confidence.
- What is the difference between being confident and being conceited?
- Why would others want to follow you or listen to you as a leader?
- What can you bring to this position that will not only help the organization, but the employees as well?
- What knowledge do you possess that will benefit the organization and the employees?
- What do you see as the most significant contribution you could make in the first two weeks?

Creativity

Considerations

Is this person creative in their work? Do they look for new approaches to accomplishing tasks? Do they look for innovative ways to approach systems and procedures? Can they articulate their ideas effectively to others? Do they "think outside the box?" Or do they wait for someone else to provide innovation and creativity?

Interview Questions
- Are you content with conducting your work "inside the box" or do you routinely think "outside the box?" If outside the box, give me some examples.
- Have you ever tried to solve a problem in a way that had never been done before? If so, what did you do and what was the outcome?
- Do you brainstorm with others to try to think of innovative ways to do your work? If yes, explain.
- Have you ever tried to convince a superior of doing a particular job or function in a different way? If yes, explain and what was the outcome?
- Have you ever had an employee come to you with a creative way to work? If yes, what was it, was it tried and if so, what was the outcome?

Decision Making

Considerations

Does this person have the skills and mental capacity to make competent and beneficial decisions, based upon the needs of the organization? Can they think competently and thoroughly? Are they efficient and timely in their decisions and avoid acting too slowly or quickly? Or are they reluctant or afraid to make decisions or do they become incapacitated?

Interview Questions

- ▶ Do you consider yourself a good decision-maker? If yes, what makes you a good decision-maker?
- ▶ Do you like to consult with others when making tough decisions? Explain pros & cons to answer.
- ▶ Tell me of a time when you had to make an important decision that couldn't wait, what was it and what was the outcome?
- ▶ Tell me of a time when you had to make a decision for something that was not your immediate responsibility and what was the outcome?
- ▶ Tell me of a time when you put off making a decision until a later time, what was it, what were the factors that led to postponing it and what was the eventual outcome?
- ▶ What process do you use or factors that you consider when making decisions?
- ▶ How long does your decision-making process usually take?

Delegation

Considerations

Is this person able to determine the potential and capacity of others and effectively delegate tasks to others within their capacity to accomplish them? Do they use delegation as a tool in developing others? Do they make assignments with deadlines, including periodic reporting and accountability? Do they know how to manage tasks? Or is this person reluctant or afraid to delegate work that needs to be done that can be accomplished through others?

Interview Questions
- ▶ Is delegation an integral part of your leadership style? Explain.
- ▶ How do you decide what can be delegated and to whom it is delegated?
- ▶ How do you approach others to willingly accept additional delegated tasks and assignments?
- ▶ What do you do to ensure that work that is delegated to others is accomplished on schedule?
- ▶ Tell me of a time when you delegated tasks to another person for the purpose of developing that person.
- ▶ Tell me of a time when delegated work was not completed on schedule and what was the outcome?

Detail Oriented

Considerations

Does this person have an awareness of and commitment to producing a quality product or service? Do they use the appropriate procedures, tools, technologies and resources in a systematic way to ensure quality? Are they concerned with every detail involved in producing quality results and know where to go if questions or concerns arise? Or do they take a casual approach to their work, that "close enough" is acceptable.

Interview Questions
- ▶ Is attention to detail important to you? Explain and give examples.
- ▶ What's the difference between quality and perfection?
- ▶ Tell me of a time when using the appropriate procedures, tools, technologies and resources resulted in superior work.
- ▶ Tell me of a time when not using the appropriate procedures, tools, technologies and resources resulted in inferior work.
- ▶ Tell me of a time when someone in your department or your organization delivered a product or service that wasn't quality. What was it, how or what caused it happen and what was the outcome?

Determination

Considerations

Does this person have a desire to stick to a task through its completion without giving up? Do they overcome hurdles and obstacles without significant delays or complications? Are they able to persevere in spite of problems? Do they possess passion for their work and their personal accomplishments? Or do they easily give up or depend upon others to help finish the job?

Interview Questions

- Do you consider yourself as having determination to see a job through? If yes, give examples.
- Tell me of a time when you had to rely solely upon yourself to accomplish a major task, what was it, what did you do and what was the outcome?
- Tell me of a time when you felt you were right about something and had to speak up and push for your position, what was it and what was the outcome?
- What is your most significant accomplishment that required determination and perseverance?
- What can you do to help others see the importance of being determined to see a job through?

Developmental Skills

Considerations

Is this person capable of training others, not only in job duties, but in developing self-leadership in others. Do they lead by example and motivation, looking for the good in others? Do they show what good performance is and then expect it? Or do they leave others to figure it out on their own or expect them to get help from others?

Interview Questions

- Is it important to you that others develop and improve their job skills? Explain.
- Who's job is it to ensure that all employees are provided with

the resources needed to improve?
- What have you done to help others develop and improve their technical skills on the job?
- What have you done to help others develop and improve their self-leadership mentality and skills?
- How do you deal with employees who aren't interested in improving themselves in their work?
- Tell me of a time when you personally tutored another employee that visibly improved their skills or performance.

Diplomacy

Considerations
Is this person capable of handling and resolving situations without arousing hostilities or ill feelings? Are they even tempered and able to take criticism while keeping their ego in check? Are they able to negotiate differences involving themselves or others to an amicable conclusion? Or do they lack the talent or resourcefulness to resolve differences diplomatically or calmly?

Interview Questions
- How would you describe "diplomacy?"
- Do you take criticism personally, even when it is intended to be personal? Explain.
- What is the difference between diplomacy and debate?
- Tell me of a time where you resolved a difficult situation using diplomacy, without creating any hostilities or ill feelings between the people involved.
- Tell me of a time when you have taken a negative situation and resolved it amicably.
- Tell me of a time when someone attacked your character or credibility, how you handled it and what was the outcome?

Ethics

Considerations
Does this person have the inner fortitude to do what is right and stand on the side of truth at all times? Do they understand the

professional standards required and have an unwavering commitment to them? Do they do what's right at all times or only when someone is watching them? Or are they willing to rationalize their ethics based upon conditions or circumstances?

Interview Questions
- ▶ How do you maintain the regulations, laws and ethical standards of our industry?
- ▶ What is your role in maintaining and fostering ethics in the workplace?
- ▶ Tell me of a time when you were faced with an ethical dilemma, what was it, what did you do and what was the outcome?
- ▶ Tell me of a time when another person was encouraging you to do something that was unethical, what was it, what did you do and what was the outcome?
- ▶ Tell me of a time when you went above and beyond the call of duty in order to avoid being involved in something illegal, unethical or against regulations.
- ▶ Have you ever witnessed another person doing something illegal, unethical or against regulations? If yes, what was it, what did you do and what was the outcome?

Judgment

Considerations
Can this person analyze the cause of a problem based upon relevant information? Can they quickly and properly evaluate personal motives and agendas of others? Do they use balanced and objective reasoning to logically evaluate problems? Or is this person easily distracted, not analytical, unable to determine relevant information, emotional or not objective?

Interview Questions
- ▶ What do you feel are the most important aspects of making good judgments?
- ▶ How can you tell if something is ineffective, needs a solution and how do you decide how to fix it?

- ▶ Tell me of a time when something needed to be corrected immediately, what did you do and what was the outcome?
- ▶ Tell me of a time when another person's work was adversely affecting your work, what was it, what did you do about it and what was the outcome?
- ▶ How do you make character judgments about the **character / motives / agendas** of other people?
- ▶ Tell me your character judgment of me; what kind of a person am I and what motivates me?

Leadership

Considerations
Does this person see the vision of the organization and its goals and objectives. Do they understand your vision of how those goals and objectives will be reached? Are they able to help others see the vision and catch the vision. Do they understand and and can they evaluate the individuals who make up a team? Do they want to help others become successful? Can they inspire others to achieve self-leadership? Or are they more interested in controlling and dictating what happens in the workplace?

Interview Questions
- ▶ Under what conditions are you most effective as a leader? Give examples.
- ▶ What is the outcome that you desire out of your employees?
- ▶ What makes a **good / bad** employee? Give examples.
- ▶ What is the most difficult aspect of leadership?
- ▶ Is it important for you to be in control as a leader? Explain.
- ▶ Is it important for leaders to openly acknowledge the success of others? Explain.
- ▶ Why do people need a leader and what makes you the leader that we need?
- ▶ How would you approach leading others to becoming self-leaders?

Learning Skills

Considerations

Does this person have the resourcefulness to gain knowledge and understanding through successes and failures, not only theirs, but others? Do they strive to constantly be learning work related knowledge, through their own initiative? Do they have a desire to help others learn? Do they have a desire to improve themselves professionally? Or are they content with what they have accomplished and that who they are right now is good enough?

Interview Questions
- Tell me what continuing education is and how it might be beneficial to you and to others.
- What is the last thing you learned that was beneficial to you in your career? When was it?
- What is the greatest learning experience you had from another person's **mistakes / successes**?
- What is the last thing you did to improve yourself in your career?
- Where do you see yourself in 5 years, and what will you do to ensure that?

Listening Skills

Considerations

Is this person capable of communicating effectively with others in their job related language? Are they interested in what others have to say as it relates to a productive and positive work environment? Are they good at extracting and understanding the information that others are trying to convey to them? Or are they too preoccupied with their own issues that they don't have time or don't care about what others have to say?

Interview Questions
- What does it mean to you to be a good listener?
- What do you do to encourage positive and productive communication from employees?

- Is there such as thing as a stupid question?
- How do you ensure that you understand exactly what others are trying to convey to you?
- How do you extract relevant and pertinent information from others in a beneficial way?

Motivation

Considerations
What motivates this person? Are they dedicated and have a passion for their work? Are they self-motivated to accomplish the most that can be accomplished each and every day? Are they motivated and supportive of your direction and endeavors? Are they motivated in setting and accomplishing their own goals in addition to those that have been set for them? Or are they undermining and motivated by their own ambitions or self-centered goals or agenda?

Interview Questions
- What motivates you?
- What do you do to make sure that you accomplish the most you can each and every day?
- Tell me of a time when you were motivated by a challenging task or assignment, what was it, why did it motivate you what was the outcome?
- Tell me of a time when you were given a task or assignment that did not motivate you, what was it, why didn't it motivate you and what was the outcome?
- Tell me of a time when you accomplished something that was motivated entirely by your own desire.
- Tell me of a time when you accomplished something that seemed impossible, what was it, what were the obstacles and what was the outcome?

Motivator

Considerations
Is this person a motivator of others? Do they set the pace in the

workplace by inspiring others? Do they help others focus on the positive aspects of success and accomplishment? Can they motivate others to improve their behavior and performance in a positive and constructive manner that enables others to become self-leaders? Or are they the type of person that believes that others should perform at their best because that's what they're being paid for?

Interview Questions
- ▶ Why do you think some people are not motivated?
- ▶ How do you motivate others? Give examples.
- ▶ Tell me of a time when you helped someone else get motivated about doing better work or accomplishing some task or assignment.
- ▶ Tell me of a time when you tried to motivate another person that was unsuccessful, what happened and what was the outcome?
- ▶ How do you deal with people who can't or won't be motivated to accomplish task, assignments or goals?
- ▶ Is there a point you reach where you no longer invest time into people who can't or won't be motivated? If yes, what is that point. If no, what recourse do you take?

Negotiation Skills

Considerations
Does this person possess any skills that would be useful and beneficial to the organization? Can they effectively mediate between parties to arrive at mutually beneficial conclusions? Are they willing to compromise when the results provide a win-win for the parties involved? Do they proactively foster equality and unity in their interactions with others? Or are they the type of person who watches or waits for things to happen as they may?

Interview Questions
- ▶ Do you have any negotiating skills? If yes, explain.
- ▶ What is the main objective of your negotiations?
- ▶ What is most important in negotiating – winning or fairness and

equality? Explain.
► How would successful negotiations be beneficial to our employees, team, department or organization?

People Skills

Considerations

How does this person interact with others? Are they kind, courteous and respectful of others, regardless of their position or authority? Do they see people as a valuable resource worth investing their time in? Are their people skills in harmony with your leadership philosophy and direction? Do they foster team work and a team spirit? Or are they only personable when the situation requires it?

Interview Questions
► How do you interact with **subordinates / peers / superiors**? Give examples.
► Do you solicit feedback from others?
► What are the pros & cons of soliciting feedback from others?
► Do you provide appropriate and timely feedback to others?
► What are the pros & cons of providing feedback to others?
► Are you able to see problems and difficulties from another person's perspective? How could this affect your ability to deal with others?
► Tell me of a time when you had to deal with a problem that was entirely a personality problem or conflict, what was the problem, how did you handle it and what was the outcome?
► What is the most important thing you've learned from a subordinate or peer?

Potential

Considerations

Does this person have the desire and motivation to do more and be better? Have they progressed and improved in the past, and if so, how? Do they have what it will take to progress within the organization and take on additional responsibilities and assignments? Can they reach higher levels of performance and success? Or will they be at their maximum potential immediately?

Interview Questions
- ▶ What is your potential worth to the **team / department / organization**? Explain and give examples.
- ▶ Where were you professionally 5 years ago? What has changed between then and now?
- ▶ Where will you be professionally 5 years from now? What will change between now and then, and what will be the catalyst of the changes you see for yourself?
- ▶ What makes you different from everybody else on the street who wants to get ahead?
- ▶ What is your greatest **asset / liability**?

Problem Solving

Considerations
Is this person a cognitive thinker who is able to see problems and applicable solutions? Do they have analytical skills and the ability to find creative and effective solutions to problems? Are they proactive in listening, watching and identifying issues, and resolving them before they become problems? Do they deal with and solve problems in a calm and determined manner? Or is this person unable to identify and solve problems without significant effort or disruption?

Interview Questions
- ▶ What information do you gather about a problem in order to solve it?
- ▶ What experience, education or skills do you have that assists you in solving problems?
- ▶ Tell me of the last problem that you solved and what could have been done differently to have prevented it from occurring or minimized its affects.
- ▶ How would you solve problems relating to **tardiness / absenteeism / motivation / team work / adherence to**

standards / adherence to policies / gossip / drama / work ethic?
▶ How do you treat the people involved in problems?
▶ What steps do you take to minimize interruptions in the work place when resolving problems?

Results Oriented

Considerations

Is this person looking for results at the end of the day? Do they help others to desire the same results? Are results an integral aspect of the performance standards? Do they establish periodic reporting of projects to ensure results? Do they want to see steady progress toward the achievement of goals and objectives? Or are they content to simply show up every day and wait for things to take care of themselves?

Interview Questions
▶ What does it mean to you to be "results oriented?" Give examples.
▶ What steps do you take personally to achieve the results expected of you by others? Give examples.
▶ What steps do you take to ensure achievable results in subordinates? Give examples.
▶ How do you know at any given time whether you're on track with your desired results?
▶ How do you know at any give time whether your subordinates are on track with their desired results?

Sales Skills

Considerations

Does this person have previous sales skills that would be useful to the organization? Are they able to sell themselves to others, and can they convey their own assets and benefits? Are they convincing to others and have the ability to get others to see their points of view? Or are they introverted or withdrawn, not concerned with getting others interested?

Interview Questions
- What is the difference between selling and marketing?
- How could our organization benefit from your **sales / marketing experience / expertise**?
- What ideas do you have that could be marketed in a way that would be beneficial to the **team / department / organization**?
- What characteristics are essential to a good **sales person / marketer**?
- How do you get others to see your point of view and convince them of your "pitch?"
- Do you feel that it would be best to market the company or the products and services?
- What attracts you to **sales / marketing** and what motivates you to achieve quantifiable results?
- On a scale of 1 to 10, where 10 is the best, how would you rate yourself as a **sales person / marketer**? Explain.
- How would you go about **selling / marketing** our organization, who would you target and what would be your strategy?
- What makes you better than every other "Joe" **sales person / marketer** out there on the streets?

Strategic Thinking

Considerations
Does this person have the ability to envision innovative and creative methods and procedures to positively impact the operation? Are they proactive in anticipating things that will affect the workplace? Are they able to plan ahead, anticipate the changes needed and resources required to implement new ideas? Or do they just wait for things to be mandated or changes to happen on their own?

Interview Questions
- How would you describe "strategic thinking?"
- If you were going to be in charge of implementing a new computerized system in the department, briefly outline what steps would you take to create a strategy?

- ▶ Why do you think that big changes are often difficult in the initial stages of implementation and what would you do differently to ensure a smooth transition throughout changes?
- ▶ Tell me of a time when you knew a change was coming that affected you and/or your department, what happened, what did you do and what was the outcome?

Strength
Considerations
Does this person have the physical, mental and emotional strength (within the confines of any legally mandated accommodations, if applicable) to succeed in the position for which they are being considered? Do they overcome difficulties and obstacles easily and positively? Do they have a dogged determination to unwaveringly see all goals, objectives, assignments and duties through to completion? Or does this person have weaknesses in any of these areas that could manifest itself as a weakness or liability at a later time?

Interview Questions
- ▶ The duties of the <<*describe the position and duties*>> can be very demanding, both physically and mentally. How do you think you'll be able to handle the demands of the job? Explain and give examples.
- ▶ Would you consider yourself as a "workaholic?" Explain.
- ▶ What is the difference between a "workaholic" and a committed employee?
- ▶ How do you maintain the stamina to get through a long and difficult day of work?
- ▶ What do you do to "recharge" yourself and keep from being over worked, overwhelmed and burned out?
- ▶ Does demanding work or long hours make you irritable or upset?
- ▶ Tell me of a time when you were faced with difficulties and challenges to accomplish your work and you overcame, what was it, what did you do and what was the outcome?

Task Management

Considerations
Does this person manage their duties and assignments without supervision? Do they avoid taking on responsibilities that belong to others? Do they ensure that their subordinates are managing their tasks as well, without taking on any additional or needless tasks? Can they effectively delegate assignments and tasks to the appropriate recipients? Do they hold others accountable to their assigned tasks? Or does this person lack a legitimate accountability system within themselves or others, where tasks and assignments are considered optional?

Interview Questions
▶ How would you describe "task management."
▶ What's the difference between task management and micro management?
▶ Should people being assigned additional tasks be given additional power or authority? Explain.
▶ How should tasks be assigned and their eventual completion be managed?
▶ Tell me of a time when you took on tasks that should have been completed by another person, what were the tasks, what happened and what was the outcome?
▶ How do you assign accountability along with the task to others?
▶ Is the completion of additional tasks and assignments necessary or optional?

Time Management

Considerations
Does this person have a plan each day for completing their tasks in a timely manner? Do they avoid wasteful activities and chatter with others? Are they realistic in the amount of time that is spent on duties and assignments? Do they instill in others a realistic awareness to time and time standards? Do they instill time management in others by example? Or do they go through the day without much regard to time except for "quitting time?"

Interview Questions
- ▶ How do you describe "time management."
- ▶ Do you practice time management? Explain and give examples.
- ▶ What are the most important things to consider when managing your time each day?
- ▶ Tell me of a time when you were given way too much time to accomplish a task or assignment, what was it and why was it too much time?
- ▶ Tell me of a time when you were not given enough time to accomplish a task or assignment, what was it and why was it not enough much time?
- ▶ Have you ever had an occasion where you finished all your work and had extra time on your hands? Explain.
- ▶ How do you instill time management in others?
- ▶ In what ways are you an example to others of effective time management?

Willingness

Considerations
Is this person willing to do whatever is required to get the job done? Are they anxious to help out when needed? Do they take changes in stride without any hesitation or resentment? Will they go the extra mile when and where it's needed? Or are they the type of person who's only willing to put in the minimal amount of time and hurries out the door at quitting time?

Interview Questions
- ▶ How do you describe "willingness."
- ▶ Tell me of a time when you were willing to go above and beyond the call of duty and help the team to accomplish something important, what was it, what did you do, what was the outcome?
- ▶ Tell me of a time when another person was unwilling to go above and beyond the call of duty and help the team to accomplish something important, what was it, what did you do,

what was the outcome?
▶ What do you do to foster a willing spirit in others?

* * * Important Legal Issues * * *

Various federal, state, and local laws regulate the questions that a prospective employer may ask an applicant. All questions asked, whether they appear on the employment application, during the interview or involved with any subsequent testing processes must be related specifically to the job for which the applicant is applying. To not hire an applicant based upon any of the following criteria (i.e. factors) is considered discriminatory;

- Nationality / National Origin / Birthplace / Race / Color
- Gender / Sex
- Religion / Religious Affiliations
- Age / Birth Date
- Disability / Health & Physical Abilities
- Marital / Family Status

However, there are questions that can be asked concerning the above criteria, so long as they are within the parameters of what is considered legal. For example, it is illegal to ask, "how old are you?" But it is not illegal to ask, "are you over the age of 18?"

Because this is an important issue with serious legal ramifications, great care and diligence should be given to this matter. Make sure that you understand what questions / types of questions are illegal and avoid them at all cost. Make your hiring decisions based upon legal criteria.

Consult with your organization's human resources department or legal department if you have any questions or concerns. If you come up against a unique situation, seek the help of others who are qualified to assist you, because, as they say, "it is better to be safe than sorry!"

SAMPLE Critical Factor Review Sheet

Applicant: Jane Doe **Position:** Payroll Asst.

Critical Factor	Weight	x	Applicant's Score	=	Total Value
Attitude	1	x	8	=	8
Cooperation	1	x	9	=	9
Customer Service	2	x	8	=	16
Dependability	1.5	x	5	=	7.5
Experience	0.5	x	8	=	4
Honesty & Integrity	3	x	6	=	18
Job Knowledge	1	x	9	=	9
Manageability	1	x	8	=	8
Personality	1.5	x	10	=	15
Safety	1	x	9	=	9
Scheduling	1.5	x	8	=	12
Sense of Urgency	1	x	7	=	7
Applicant's Overall Score:					**122.5**

Notes: I'm concerned about her dependability, took an excessive number of days off from previous job that weren't absolutely necessary. She has a bubbly and energetic personality - very likable. She has lots of experience and knowledge – wouldn't need a lot of training and hand holding. There seemed to be an issue about missing office supplies at her previous job where she was accused of taking them home with her. She tried to avoid the issues and I had to ask repeatedly to get the story out of her. She shrugged it off as a non-issue, but it doesn't set well with me.

Interviewer: Tracey Culbertson   **Date:** 11/16/2006

In this example, twelve factors were considered (you can have as few / many as you need) for scoring the applicant's interview.

(1) The critical factors are listed in the first column.

(2) The weight of the factor is entered in the second column. In this example, it can be seen that "Customer Service" is twice as important to the interviewer (weight of 2) as is "Attitude" and "Cooperation" (weight of 1 ea.), but not as important as "Honesty & Integrity" (weight of 3).

(3) The applicant's score (on a scale of 0-10, where 10 is the best) is entered in the 4th column (as determined by the interviewer).

(4) The total (Weight X Applicant's Score) is entered in the right column and the individual totals are totaled at the bottom, giving an overall score.

(5) A section at the bottom of the page is available for additional notes to be added to the review sheet by the interviewer.

A system like this could be used routinely in the interviewing and hiring practice. It would be a permanent record of the interviewer's initial reactions to the applicant's answers, providing a meaningful and quantifiable assessment. It would be especially useful when multiple people are interviewing the same applicants.

At the end of the interview process, the interviewers could review applicants, compare notes, tally scores and determine the best candidate, based upon specific criteria.

ADVERTISEMENT

Effective leaders are those who are innovative and consistently think outside the box. When the work is done and it's time to have fun, why should you be confined to limitations and restrictions designed to keep you thinking and playing inside the box?!

Finally, a game that let's you *think and play outside the box*!

"Oh My Word"

brand word / card game

Most traditional games confine you to a game board, cube, grid or a box. Not any more! With **"Oh My Word,"** there are no physical confines, no boards, no grids, no cubes, and definitely no boxes!

Don't waste lots of time staring at a board, cube, grid or a box looking for a way to make a play! Don't let your opponents box you in or out! Liberate yourself to focus on playing the game, not staring at the playing field! **"Oh My Word"** plays without a game board, cube, grid or box! The possibilities for game play are virtually endless and limited only by your imagination!

"Oh My Word" is not just one game, but is **6 games in 1**! You can play any of the six games with the same cards! One of the most fun and exciting games ever created is ***Battle of Words*** and is not available anywhere else on the planet! In addition, you can play ***Standard Crossword***, ***3-D Crossword***, ***Word Search***, ***Word Jumble*** and ***Word Solitaire-*** that's 6 games for the price of 1!

Don't be the last kid on the block to have it! Get yours now and give some as gifts at: **MAXnJAX.com/OhMyWord**

www.ingramcontent.com/pod-product-compliance
Lightning Source LLC
Chambersburg PA
CBHW071417170526
45165CB00001B/309